AS OTHERS SEE US

Body Movement and the Art of Successful Communication

Ellen Goldman

Routledge
Taylor & Francis Group

NEW YORK AND LONDON

Published in 2004 by
Routledge
711 Third Avenue
New York, NY 10017, USA

Published in Great Britain by
Routledge
2 Park Square, Milton Park Abingdon,
Oxon OX14 4RN

Routledge is an imprint of the Taylor & Francis Group, an informa business

Library of Congress Cataloging-in-Publication Data

Goldman, Ellen
  As others see us : body movement and the art of successful communication / Ellen Goldman.
    p. cm.
  Includes bibliographical references and index.
    ISBN 0-415-94918-1 (pbk.)
    1.Body language. 2. Nonverbal communication. I. Title.
BF637.N66G65 2003
153.6'9—dc22   2003063013

AS OTHERS SEE US

Ellen Goldman is a leader in the field of movement analysis, having made the study of movement her life's work. Early dance training led to an avid interest in choreography, performance and the establishment of a dance company. She helped found New York's respected Laban/Bartenieff Institute of Movement Studies. Ellen is considered a central force in Laban Movement Analysis which includes body, effort and space training to ensure the full expression of the mover.

Ellen has been a member of Action Profilers International since 1980 and has served for ten years on the General Council. The Action Profiling® System, developed in England, analyzes movement patterns in everyday communication to demonstrate inherent personal preferences that lead to different ways of thinking and acting.

Her interest in research and development has led to a collaboration with Dr. Deborah DuNann Winter, testing theories of the Action Profiling System. In addition, Ellen expanded her skills and theoretical knowledge by training in the Kestenberg Movement Profile, a system based on the study of movement paralleling psychanalytic theory as it applies to childhood development. Together with Dr. Judith Kestenberg, she has been studying the Laban scales of movement in the context of communication.

In workshops and courses throughout the U.S. and abroad, Ellen's innovative methods continue to demonstrate the influence of body movement in our daily lives.

To my family, Ralph and Anna,
for their tolerance and encouragement

Acknowledgement

The author wishes to acknowledge the collaboration and contribution of Pamela Ramsden which was critical to the conception and development of AS OTHERS SEE US.

Special Thanks

Special thanks to Patricia Millman for her subtlety and sensitivity while editing AS OTHERS SEE US and to Rachael Bickhardt for her persistence and skill in the preparation of this book.

Additional Thanks

To the many friends and colleagues who discusses their lives and work with me; to the participants of workshops who trusted and explored these ideas. To the Laban Institute for the many opportunities it offered me, as faculty, and for maintaining a home for the Laban work. To my teachers, Irmgard Bartenieff, Warren Lamb, Pamela Ramsden, Bonnie Bainbridge Cohen, Dr. Judith Kestenberg, and many others who opened doors to a new reality and gave me a chance to dedicate myself to the love of movement. To Ronnie Carson and Marion Weinstein for their support throughout the writing process of this book. To Sculpture Placement, Ltd. for their generosity in providing the many photographs of J. Seward Johnson, Jr.'s works which appear throughout this book.

CONTENTS

O wad some Power the giftie gie us
To see oursels as ithers see us!
It wad frae mony a blunder free us,
    An' foolish notion:
What airs in dress an' gait wad lea'e us,
    An' ev'n devotion!

Robert Burns
To A Louse

PROLOGUE

By opening this book you have embarked on a journey to the interior of the art of communication. My goal in writing this book is to help you become aware of your own continuous stream of body movement and to enable you to experience the subtleties of body language. I hope you will go beyond a superficial observation of movement to a skill which encompasses the whole person, the context and yourself. Ultimately, you will become a kind of kinesthetic mirror of what you observe.

Once you understand the connection between your physical behavior and what is on your mind, you can explain difficult thoughts easily, and comfortably express feelings which might have been left unspoken. The interplay of the physical and intellectual will provide a full and engaging experience of communication.

The suggestions and exercises in this book will awaken a new level of perception in you, one which will give you choices and knowledge of what is happening in the moment. You can then tell if you are facilitating communication or inadvertently impeding it. Some people will want to master the process in depth. For others, a general sense will be enough. Yet even a general awareness of movement will create a recognition for the meaning behind words and an appreciation for the non-verbal aspects of communication.

You do not need to change how you dress or walk or talk. Our methods do not advocate changing behavior to "get" something: the man, the job, money, but they do remove inconsistencies which might be in your way. All that is required is a deep level of listening and self-observation. You will need to experiment with what is not obvious or blatant. You may think you understand gestures now, and you probably do. But you will learn to question your interpretation and expand your knowledge. You will even have insights about your own communication which may be very revealing.

In the earliest developmental stages of this book, my colleague Pamela Ramsden and I decided to use our knowledge of Integrated Movement in our own communication. This had never been done before. Previously, we observed Integrated Movement identifying its components, and used our findings to analyze decision-making. The method is called The Action Profile® System.[1] Then we discovered that we could use Integrated Movement in the flow of communication as an important new way to give feedback to each other.

We thought of the verbal statement as the last step in a longer process which started in the body. We referred to the presence or absence of Integrated Movement, reflecting on what that meant to our verbal statement.

As we talked about the usual topics between friends, rather than giving advice, we said, *"that's a gesture,"* or *"that's a posture."* To us, this meant that we had not yet gotten to the core of the issue. We also said, *"why didn't you take a stand* (a posture) on *that, and say what you wanted?"*

We learned to check our own non-verbal signals. A slouching posture might tell me I have given up inside, though I have said I am determined to finish. My own physical experience could contradict my belief that I had it all under control.

In this book I hope you will learn to do what we did, to take a problem, stop, identify it, analyze the pieces, then coax each other into Integrated Movement solutions. The process of observation itself assists in creating clarity for oneself and acceptance of others. Careful observation wipes away stereotypes and lets us see the unity of mind and body in the other person and in ourselves.

Pam and I experimented with each process ourselves, presented the ideas in workshops, noted reactions and experiences. We instructed the mind and watched what the body did naturally; we instructed the body and watched the results in communication. This book will teach you how to do the same.

Casual conversations with friends became opportunities to experiment. I introduced colleagues to the technique and asked them to report back to me. Over the course of more than five years, I tested the principles, designed experiments for students, and challenged myself and others to describe the experiences of posture, gesture and Integrated Movement as they happened.

As Others See Us breaks the process down into easy steps. Its descriptions will give you a sense of what others have done, so that you will develop an awareness just from picturing the experience in your mind's eye. You may wish to work with a friend so you can try the ideas yourself and develop your own skills.

As my skills grew, I found I could improve poor communication by observing and questioning what I saw and felt. You will be able to do this too. There were major insights and great disappointments, but I learned how to contact the real me. This became a treasure which I want to share with you. It is both satisfying and useful to be able to pinpoint and articulate your own experience. It is a skill you cannot lose. I learned that knowledge, not yet in my mind, was in my body. And my body would alert me to take a deeper look. I learned to express myself more easily and communicate more succinctly and clearly.

The awareness will become second nature. At any inkling of trouble, tension, emotion in yourself or in someone else, you can draw on these techniques to break the old pattern and create choice. It is a freedom I value tremendously and I am sure you will too.

The approach is analytic in that you become an observer. It is also intuitive as you trust the experience of the moment. In this way, you bridge the dream and waking reality by bringing your internalized images to life. This method works comfortably with other body-mind methods, such as visualization, and adds to their depth.

The value of this book lies mainly in the process it presents. I have not tried to prove a theory but to develop awareness and practical skills. As you read this book, I hope you will experiment with these ideas and test them for yourself. At some point, you may notice with surprise that the link between movement and communication has become obvious and the benefits easily within reach.

ONE

PERCEIVING MOVEMENT

Movement equals survival. Without the common adaptations we automatically make to our surroundings we could feel lost in a frightening and alien environment[1]. For instance, it would be impossible to be aware of all of the elements of perception we need to perform even a simple task like crossing a street. It takes an amazing amount of perceptual skill just to estimate speed of approaching cars and regulate our response.

There are several specific experiments designed to give us an appreciation of the complexities of perception. One is called *The Crooked Room*[2], in which everything is crooked: the floor, the walls, the furniture. When we are in this room, we can feel our inner sensation struggling to keep balance and to make sense of the experience. When we leave, the 'real world' seems distorted and scrambled but just for a while, until the steady feedback of the environment convinces us to return to normal.

In our personal universe, each of us experiences ourselves as the center. We are each like the sun, and all of the objects in our environment relate to us. But we depend on our environment to provide us with a sense of movement.

To experience this, the next time you walk down a tree-lined street, try to notice the alternation of parallel movement in the rows of trees and buildings in your visual field. Whatever is closest to you will seem to move backward, while the next row of trees seems to travel with you[3].

On the largest scale, if we imagined ourselves in outer space observing the earth, human movement would become insignificant. Yet within the sphere of our own lives it's importance is monumental. Our perception is very selective. We cannot simultaneously experience all movement at once. The result is that ever-present movement and movement on vastly different scales tend to drop out of our perception. Remember, our planet is spinning at a rate of 800 miles per hour, while speeding around the sun at 60,000 miles per hour in a solar system that is itself speeding through space[4]. We do not experience the movement of our planet because we have no background against which to judge it. In fact, what is constant and consistent, and moves without any fixed background, or fixed point of reference, will eventually slip from awareness.

Nevertheless, we can choose to become aware of many of the changing aspects of movement. To do so, we may need to first disturb our familiar perceptions, our comfortable skills, in order to momentarily experience the complexity of our environment. Otherwise we might insist that what we see is all there is, seriously limiting our knowledge.

In our first few years of life we quickly learn how to manipulate our environment through movement; what to expect from our environment; how it will respond to us and what we can do to affect it. This is a common, shared experience for every person on this planet, so common that we take it almost totally for granted.

Our movement serves the function of telling us where we are in space. It allows us to learn to cope with the incredibly complex environment around us. The process is part of who we are and who we become. As we reach, push, pull, stretch, turn, stand, sit, as we develop from infants to adults, we learn and define patterns which will serve us in functional and expressive ways. No wonder, some parts of communication will always be expressed more easily and naturally in movement than in words.

In non-verbal communication, researchers who have studied movement looked selectively at the human body. Some people watched gestures, some watched postures, positions, eye blinks, eye directions, pointing. Some watched patterns and phrases between people; things like rhythmicity and synchronicity, initiations, interruptions and frequency of speech[5]. As in all observation, the choice of what is observed shapes the result.

We can watch the joints and the changing parts of the body contrasting and shifting in counterpoint and polyrhythm. These are GESTURES and will tell us about signs and descriptions. . . .a woman nods her head in acknowledgment as she reaches to shake hands. We can watch the total body assume shapes and poses. These are POSTURES and will tell us about attitudes and roles. . . . a man casually leans against the wall waiting to meet someone. Or we can see a flow of movement spread equally throughout the body, like the perfected movement of an athlete making a tennis serve. This is called an INTEGRATED MOVEMENT, a movement which until now has been neglected in our awareness.

When the limbs and torso are moving together, neither the posture nor the gesture draws attention. The Integrated Movement becomes less obvious and seems to disappear into the background. Thus, Integrated Movement seems ephemeral. One is almost not sure it has happened. Like a shooting star or a moving wave, it is fleeting. But when Integrated Movement has occurred, a deeply held thought or feeling, even a statement of one's world view, has been expressed. Something valuable has happened in human communication which bypasses the concerns, details, distractions of daily life in favor of a broader, deeper meaning. A door has been opened in communication.

We tend to be swept into the feelings conveyed by the movement and lose awareness of all else. It will take a shift of perception to bring Integrated Movement into awareness, a shift which may temporarily disturb our excellent faculties of perception. But then, as we learn to 'see' movement, more and more of human interaction will become visible. We will be rewarded because the seemingly inflexible positions and unresolved conflicts will become negotiable and amenable to change.

In his satiric poem, "To A Louse," Robert Burns graphically describes an elegant lady sitting proudly in church while a louse crawls on her bonnet. How frustrating to be so vulnerable to other people's observation and so cut off from our own. There are gaps between how we see ourselves and how others see us which leave too much room for error and misunderstanding. We can change this. If every time we moved we generated a substance like a spider spinning a web, we would see that our conversation itself would have us wrapped in a gigantic Gordian Knot. Imagine that the knot is a beautiful tapestry, the crossings and loopings providing an individualized design of how we create our living experience.

TWO

LOOKING AT MOVEMENT: GESTURES AND POSTURES

Human expression, sometimes mysterious and complex, sometimes simple and basic, is always a perfect unity. Some of us express ourselves in a pragmatic way, others creatively. Some reactions may be spontaneous, others elaborately planned. Yet, every reaction is an automatic combination of mind and body linked in a perfect partnership.

We humans may look very much alike to a citizen from another planet but in our own eyes, we are unique. When we study body, mind and movement, we are defining our unique differences of expression.

We think of the mind as an independent source of thought and inspiration. The physical participation of our body in our mental processes is less obvious to us.

Try this: close your eyes. Concentrate on feeling the movement of your body as you breathe. You may become sensitive to the sounds outside, the temperature of the room, the position of your arms and legs, which you may not have noticed before.

Through our bodies we perceive our environment and instantly interpret it. For example, a hungry body keeps the mind focused on food; the sound of an animal moving in the bushes rivets your attention; you catch a falling crystal vase and save it from smashing.

Often when we close our eyes and relax, our minds wander to chores, memories or imagined dialogues. We are all familiar with this process. We know that the mind is free to roam unfettered by practical needs; I can travel to China in my thoughts and not need any transportation, visa, money or luggage. I am free to imagine anything I want, without limit. The body, while not as fanciful a traveler, is a reliable indicator of the workings of the mind. Thus, by observing the body we can gain access to hidden thoughts and beliefs, even to patterns of behavior in which we function but which are locked away in storage, operative, but out of awareness.

The body expresses feelings in different ways: a flick of an eyebrow; a jump for joy; a clenched fist. It takes complex coordination of body and mind, postures and gestures, to permit us to look meek and fearful; to look bold and tough. The body/mind process works together conscientiously. The partnership is so perfect it allows us to know what we want and organize to act in appropriate ways.

From the first awareness of a desire or need we organize our resources, our talents, our training towards satisfying that need. We get help from friends or professionals, so that we can take each step, grow, and fulfill the blueprint of our lives. If we have difficulty applying our energy toward accomplishing our goals, we can look for clues by examining movement. Old patterns may be continually repeating. The pattern could become a static physical posture, bringing rigidity into the process; into a relationship, into work habits and self-images.

When this happens, verbal information is inadequate. It continually describes the existing condition without progressing.

Analyzing a situation using words alone loses much of the variation of feeling and subtlety of the situation. It is like trying to tell the color of a flower from the seed. Movement will have the richness of color, texture and shape to provide the additional information we need.

The word 'mind' can have a global meaning: the consciousness of humankind, the collective unconscious, the Mind of the Universe. In our usage here, the word "mind" encompasses the body. The body becomes a way of entering into various states of mind. We can change our "mind" through attention to the body.

The body and mind are always in total, instantaneous touch with each other. The body represents us in our journey through time and space. With body and mind working together as partners we are free to explore our life circumstances, who we are, what opportunities we have, what we can create, what we can discard. We are free to experience ourselves and others. We are beginning a journey of understanding and change.

GESTURES AND POSTURES GO HAND IN HAND

Gestures and Postures are the frequent, continuous movement changes that happen in the body while speaking, walking, even sleeping. It is critical to understand the differences between postures and gestures in our study of movement. Postures are the activity of the whole body at once.

Postures are the more static and unchanging aspects of movement; they provide us with stability and consistency. They reinforce our behaviors such as: *"I am friendly, thoughtful, lively, cautious." "I am a good mother, friend, lover." "I am successful, wealthy, unhappy, dejected."* We have taught ourselves to project certain attitudes and we recognize ourselves in these postures. Postures develop from parental attitudes in upbringing, from role-models and from reactions to life events.[1] We copy and learn postures. We store these in our bodies and use them to convey our desires and intentions. Postures are reactions to beliefs and statements of others as well as projections of our own beliefs.

Gestures are different. They are the expression of adaptations of *parts* of the body, not the whole body. Gestures are vital to us for ordinary activities like making our morning coffee, waving 'hello,' dismissing things with a shrug, and generally getting along. Some gestures are like signatures, they are so completely, individually ours. They may look decorative, extraneous or merely silly, but invariably they are significant. They help us sequence our verbal communication and layer it with messages. We record this information at a glance and automatically adjust to it.

Whereas gestures establish and keep the beat between people, giving a coherent rhythm to communication, postures support communication and establish a common platform of meaning. Without this underlying coordination of movements, we would have a hard time communicating.

We do not consciously keep track of these rhythms or shapes because we do not need to, but we should recognize them and understand what they represent. In these patterns we see compatibility, affiliations, group cohesion. There is as much under the surface of communication as there is above!

Since communication is what this book is about, take a moment now to do these easy exercises with a friend. You'll see, perhaps to your surprise, how often you use postures and gestures and how revealing they can be.

Discovering Your Personal Postures and Gestures

Gestures:

Try mimicking a friend's gestures while maintaining a conversation. Become familiar with your friend's gestures.

Note how they enhance your understanding of the communication. Discuss them with your friend and agree on their meaning.

Let your friend mimic your gestures. You are now creating a personal dictionary of gestures and their meaning.

Postures:

Practice playing a role just for fun. Take on the arguments of your adversary. Feel your state of mind change and be aware of how your posture changes.

Life-size bronze sculpture titled, "No Hands"

ALL ABOUT GESTURES

Each body part has its own way of moving. Each part transmits a signal, communicates, generates activity. Each part of the body can make learned, symbolic and expressive statements.

> Close your eyes and picture a part of your body; for instance, your right hand. Move it around. See how it feels. As you move this part of your body, what might you be thinking, saying or doing?

SYMBOLIC GESTURES

Most parts of our body are loaded with associations and meanings, sexual connotations, secret signs and standard messages. It is traditional to wave with a hand gesture; rub the stomach to say 'I'm full'; or spread the arms to welcome someone. Many gestures are cues between people to begin or end conversations.

Some gestures are signals. My father shakes his teacup to say, *"Fill it up, please"*; two therapists always light their pipes synchronously (unconsciously) before an important intervention.[2] Families and groups establish rules which are enacted in gestures. People attach personal meaning to their own gestures and learn to understand each other's. Thus, gestures both participate in the structure of communication and have personal meanings.

FUNCTIONAL GESTURES

We also use gestures to perform habitual tasks and chores which do not need our total physical or emotional commitment. With gestures we change the TV channel and water the plants. Any activity where we divide our attention and do more than one thing at a time, is done with gestures. When we are unsure of ourselves we test the situation by using gestures. *"Do you mind if I sit here?,"* we say with a point of the head, when we need to share a table at a cafeteria. *"Let me try that,"* we say as we take over putting carrots into a new food processor. Movement, when it is being learned, is a series of gestures. Grace and ease come later, with the confidence that a movement can be performed safely and freely.[3]

Some skills only demand gestures. For instance, an experienced knitter can easily knit and watch television at the same time. An adult doing a puzzle needs only a small gesture to insert a piece, while the child, less practiced, uses her whole body, showing a greater degree of involvement.

Gestures are the main units of communication. There are more gestures in everyone's repertoire than any other kinds of movement. And the number and variety of gestures differs greatly.

SOCIAL USE OF GESTURES

Compliments are gestures. Casual requests are usually gestures. Apologies, introductions, explanations, directions, narratives about people, places or things are important and necessary gestures.

Here are the way gestures sound:

"Hello. How are you?"

"Nice to meet you."

"I'm sorry, I never thought it would bother you."

"What a nice house."

If you think the message of the statements above is conveyed by the words alone, try making a statement with no gestures. Of course, you will have to allow the mouth to move, but do not let other parts of the body respond: no smile, no change in your eyes, no little bow of the head. You will find there is no way to totally neutralize the body except when the exchange is very mechanical, like requesting a train ticket or saying *"pass the salt."* Gestures accompanying verbal statements invariably offer additional information. *"Excuse me, do you have change for a dollar?,"* we ask as we offer the bill with a small movement of the hand and a bow of the head, apologetically. The gesture buffers the request and the stranger feels less threatened.

Sometimes when we are in a tense or uncomfortable position, an appropriate gesture has a positive effect. Saying *"I really have to go,"* with a glance at your watch helps break an overly long conversation. *"Hi, I can't talk now, I'm late for class,"* with a little skip away, helps us exit without feeling we have been abrupt.

Similarly, if you greet someone in a formal, Western cultural setting with no handshake, they will get the message that you wish to remain distant. It is a way of being cool without having to be impolite. Often we notice a gesture in the voice alone. The words: *"I'm fine"* can be said in a tone of voice dismissing any further discussion, implying *"Don't ask further." "I'm not fine but I don't want to discuss it right now."* Thus, gestures can directly contradict words. *"I love the gift,"* you say, without enthusiasm, or you raise an eyebrow to indicate that the words are not the whole story. You have leaked your true feelings. It might be preferable to say, *"I thank you for the gift. It was very thoughtful of you."* Your gesture is straightforward and you can mean what you say.

You can be sure the body will say what you feel, whether you want it to or not. Everyone feels more comfortable if what is said verbally equals what is said nonverbally. Choosing gestures carefully, you can be honest and polite.

GESTURES IN SPEECHES AND PRESENTATIONS

When delivering a speech, words alone do not convey the message. There must be a careful blend of appropriate expressive gestures to accompany the words. When gestures are too numerous, they can be confusing and distracting. The listener tends to pay more attention to the speaker's movement than to what is being said. For example, if the speaker fidgets and squirms while talking, he is engaged in a secondary communication with himself that has little to do with the text.

One can easily distinguish gestures that are referring to the self versus gestures which are going out to the audience, exposing the speaker's feelings and inviting communication. These are essential for a successful delivery. Even a brilliant text, if it is delivered with no audience contact, will most probably flop. Personal, communicative gestures are vital. Learned, rehearsed gestures are a disaster. Artificial gestures, which are not natural to the speaker, create a wall which keeps the audience from being able to empathize or even relate to the speaker.

Gestures can not only confuse an audience, they can confuse the speaker as well. A simple statement can become so embellished that it becomes unintelligible. When this happens, thoughts interrupt each other, comments are added to comments and the speaker loses track of content.

The quality of the gesture can give us valuable information about the personal style of the speaker, his feelings about the topic, or his feelings about the listener. Is the statement made with a sweep of the hand, as if the thought is being swept away, dismissed? Does it come with a jab, saying, *"Listen to this, it's important"* or *"I'm jabbing you, wake up!"* All this information is conveyed in gestures that accompany words.

THE TROUBLE WITH GESTURES

Gestures can interrupt our thought process. Your book falls to the floor. By the time you have picked it up, you've lost your idea. The idea has gotten shuffled up in the process of moving about. While this could be helpful if you

> ### Eliminate Multiple Gestures And Conflicting Ideas
>
> Take a deep breath, pause, and focus on one idea. Express it simply and clearly, vocally and in your body movement. Your voice will automatically sound like it is coming from your whole self. Stop. Say no more. You have now presented one thought with only the relevant gestures. Do not be tempted to say more. Pause. Wait. If necessary, present the next thought the same way.

are stuck and need a fresh thought, it is not helpful if you are engrossed in an important train of thought.

Some gestures are associated with tension. These include scratching the head to enhance thinking or other semiconscious, repetitive gestures people use when they are *"lost in thought."* Tongue-chewing, nail-biting kinds of gestures all express tension in one part of the body. They can help us remain engaged in the task despite other concerns. Nervousness and discomfort can be personal habits or temporary reactions. On the positive side, this tension can protect us from a threat of, or real danger. If a gesture is simply a habit, we can attempt to eliminate it.

In a one-to-one situation, the use of numerous gestures (the result of complex feelings) can interfere with direct communication. Giving instructions to a new employee, you might find numerous gestures blocking good communication. Realizing that every new employee needs simple guidelines in order to perform the job properly, you will need to clarify your expression.

Gestures alone are not powerful enough to change more complex emotional issues. Underlying attitudes have to be changed, needing a deeper commitment. Skillfully chosen gestures could start a process of change, but then the rest of the body must get involved if the change is going to be realized. Gestures can only describe the problem. But don't be discouraged, a gesture can lead you into a full commitment.

POSTURES: THE SUPER-STATEMENT

You always have a posture of some kind, be it casual, accepting, or even neutral. It is a platform from which you can gesture. Your posture can change, all at once or bit by bit. You can stretch into a new posture as you relax from a cramped position or you can move limb by limb until a new arrangement is complete.

> To see postures, picture the body as a shape emerging from its surroundings, its form making a continuous contour framed by, say, a chair, the wall or a window. Do not let your eye settle on individual parts but concentrate on the body as a sculpture outlined in space.

Life-size bronze sculpture titled, "Sidewalk Judge"

POSTURES SET THE MOOD

The whole body, arms, legs, hands, back and feet are arranged in a config-uration which projects a mood or feeling: *"I am tired,"* can be seen in a drooping body, or, *"I am listening attentively,"* seen as a focused, alert body. The posture sets the mood. It remains the same even if there are gestures accompanying it, like doodling with a pencil, taking notes as I listen, turning my head to answer your question.

The mood you find yourself in is a result of the mental image you have. Your mood will vary and so will your posture depending on whether you are telling yourself that things are *"great!"* or *"terrible."* The mental image you have creates the state of mind from which you act.

Here's an exercise that will illustrate how posture creates a mood:

Picture yourself in a lovely setting. How does your body feel to you? Relaxed and at ease or tense and alert? How would it look to some-one else? Does this mood make you more or less accessible to others?

To gain an awareness of your own postures, you need to be able to 'listen' to your thoughts, recognize the statement your thoughts would make and accept that your posture is participating in that statement. For example, if you are saying to yourself: *"That won't work, it's no good.,"* these critical thoughts will project in your posture. If you recognize this critical reaction and it is not what you want to project, you can choose to replace the critical thought with a non-critical one. Instead of *"That won't work,"* think *"What will work?"* Then you are in a helpful posture, looking for solutions. Communication is a two-way street. If it is not working, check out your postures and clear away the obstructions.

A second way to understand your posture is to actually feel it in your body and see it in your mind's eye. If you sense you are stiff, tense, holding back, see if there is something that you have not acknowledged that is causing this posture. Address the situation in a new way, rather than staying in a reactive posture. A new posture will form.

Suppose you have to attend the wedding of a distant relative on the very weekend you were planning to go to the beach. Your posture indicates annoy-ance and anger at your predicament. You create a fight with the nearest available person, just to give vent to those feelings. The fight leaves you feeling terrible and justifies your original frustration.

So what do you do? Start by acknowledging the posture. If, in fact, you must attend the wedding, set about replacing the attitude of frustration with a receptive one. Consider something positive you might gain from attending the event and allow yourself an appropriate posture. You are not fooling yourself, you are keeping an open mind. Choosing to change your body posture allows a larger perspective and more options. As a result, the situation will seem to adjust to you.

One woman made an important shift just in time to rescue a Thanksgiving dinner. She felt hurt and disappointed that her son-in-law would not be attending the family's annual Thanksgiving dinner. (The young couple had decided to separate.) The Mother's dejected posture threatened to overshadow the happy feelings she had about the event. She needed to find an appropriate way to address those feelings. In addition, she realized that her posture inadvertently undermined her daughter's difficult decision. Recognizing this, and acknowledging the difficulties, she allowed her posture to once again become warm and welcoming.

On one of my out-of-town business trips, I called my husband. He told me about taking our daughter to see The Nutcracker Suite ballet for the first time. I had such a vivid picture of them that when I hung up the telephone, I suddenly missed being there with them very much. My mental picture of them created joy, then I felt the distance from them and felt sadness. As I prepared to meet with my associates, I realized that these emotions showed in my posture. I needed an image of a productive, enjoyable meeting to be able to shift physically and mentally into an appropriate attitude for the task at hand.

Below are five steps for mastering your own personal super-statements:

1. Become aware of your posture by listening to your thoughts.
2. Evaluate these thoughts for usefulness and effectiveness.
3. If necessary, construct a new attitude.
4. Feel the change in your body.
5. Use your body posture to help generate the positive feeling.

THE BEST USE OF POSTURES

As people begin to build rapport, they tend to adopt each other's postures. Even when this is momentary, it creates a matching of attitude which promotes ease in communication. As the relationship develops further, complementary postures continue to evolve.

It might look like this: while leaning down on the arm of a chair, one person might consider an issue, while the other person expands into the space brimming full of ideas. A poised, attentive posture helps some students learn, while a relaxed, casual posture helps others. Salesmen know what reactions they are getting by being alert to the posture of the buyer. You can easily see which people in a group will be ready to participate by the availability seen in their posture.

You really need a posture when you have to object to something or defend someone. You may need to take a strong stand and you can only do it with a posture. A statement like *"Stop. That's wrong!,"* has to have a posture to match it or it is a helpless farce.

Postures are useful when practicing assertiveness or testing your position of power. Postures help charismatic leaders and spokespeople gain public support. Susan B. Anthony traveled and lectured throughout the United States and Europe in the mid 1800's insisting that women have the right to vote. Anwar Sadat risked his life promoting peace between Egypt and Israel. Martin Luther King, Jr. mobilized America against the injustices of segregation.

PREPARING FOR CONFLICT

Every relationship in work and family has its inherent status differences, personal and cultural. Some differences are fixed and some change. As the relationship changes, so do the postures. Postures naturally tend to match each other in a relationship of equals. In an argument, when postures match, they escalate the argument and make it hard to resolve. Hostility generates hostility; anger generates anger; rebellion promotes rebellion. Occasionally, in a relationship of equals, an apology for a mistake can take the wind out of the angry person's sails. Or, a bully may be shocked out of his or her bullying posture when he or she meets another bully. But when status conditions are not equal, postures generate their opposites. For example, rebellion in a teenager promotes a domineering posture in the parent; meekness promotes tyrannizing; apologetic behavior promotes accusative behavior. In unequal status relationships like this, you must equal the posture of the accuser with your own, to show that you do not accept the blame or guilt.

The physical posture keeps the thought process held within its parameters. And so the posture reinforces the argument. The posture attempts to justify itself, not to change. Common complaints can become postures and generate defensive counter-postures rather than resolution.

"We don't spend enough time together."

"You're always late."

"You never do things right."

When you notice yourself thinking in these terms or you feel a fight brewing, think about your own posture and change it.

1. Physically put yourself in a new position. Move to a new chair. Stand. Sit. Relax your body. Change your arms and legs. Move.

2. Your mind is now ready to think along a different tack. Make your statement specific and talk about your own need or fear.*"This must be done right, and there are still errors. What are you going to do?" "If we don't make time for each other we will find ourselves out of touch."*

3. Do not expect an instant response. It may take time for the other posture to dissolve. Let your statement rest and move on to other topics. The change has occurred. The results may come in later.

Your need alone may be compelling enough to generate understanding. You can stop here, or:

4. Go on to spell out a solution which would suit you.

    "I'd like to spend more time together. Let's go to the movies (a museum, a ball game, theater, etc.)"

In our relationships, we tend to focus on the other person's posture, but not on our own. We feel the other person has to change. Don't let a posture ruin your day. If it looks like it's a menace, get rid of it, any way you can. Laugh at it. Exaggerate it. Make it look ridiculous. The posture is potentially part of a chain reaction which elicits another posture. Before you know it, you are repeating the same old arguments. Instead, dissolve your posture and create a real solution.

RESOLVING CONFLICT

When a conflict sounds like this, postures are rushing out, tripping over themselves:

"You always undermine me when we are with other people," says Jane. (posture)

"No, I don't," responds Tom. (posture)

"You embarrassed me last night with Karen and Fred." (Jane intensifies her posture)

"You always criticize me." (Tom adopts a counter-posture)

We all know where this leads. Jane is taking a stand, exaggerating, generalizing and hiding what is really bothering her behind a posture. Should Tom pursue proving her wrong? Definitely not! That would only serve to escalate the situation and make Jane even more determined to prove herself right. Instead, Tom might say:

"Do you really think I always undermine you? That's not my intention. Point it out to me next time so I can see what you mean."

Assuming the good will of both parties, Tom's understanding and restraint may help clarify the real issues here. Tom could match Jane's posture, the tone, quality, size and shape of it. But he need not defend himself verbally. If his posture matches her's, non-verbally he is saying: *"You cannot intimidate me with your loud voice and angry stance, but I will deal with what's bothering you."*

To understand your participation in a conflict or disagreement you may want to replay the exchange in your mind and think about the postures and gestures that took place. Were there antagonistic postures or threatening gestures? If you were attacked, did you assume a position of defense? Did your defensive posture keep you from expressing your view of the situation?

When emotions are intense and the stakes are high, a pre-arranged set of rules may be useful. One couple I know invented this one: no one could walk out on the relationship without giving the other twenty-four hours notice. (This allowed time for reconsideration and negotiation.) Other rules, like "equal time" or "no interruptions," can give people the chance to calm down and listen to the other's point of view.

POSTURES AND THE ADULT-TEENAGER RELATIONSHIP

Teenagers seem to be able to bring out intense postures from adults. Perhaps teens are particularly sensitive to reading the nonverbal statements of their parents, as seen in postures. When dealing with children or teenagers, it is best that the adult take great care in choosing postures. If a decision made from a posture backfires, you are left with either giving up the posture or maintaining one that does not work.

Beware of dramatic changes in posture: *"You always..."* is the beginning of a statement of posture. *"You never..."* is the same. They can escalate the picture of disaster in seconds, and suddenly the whole relationship is at stake. *"If you don't let me go to the movies, it means you don't love me,"* says the teenager, setting up a posture (spoken or not). If the parent takes up the challenge and says: *"I'm the parent, obey me,"* the child either backs down or walks out. In the latter case, war is declared. Big guns are being used when small guns or no guns were needed.

Of course, teenagers need limits, but they don't need you to match their postures. In close relationships, don't fight posture with posture. Do what's necessary for each situation and let your posture serve as a support for the larger message of your love and concern.

One day my daughter wanted to meet her friends, when she had been up late with them the night before. I said *"no."* Her response was: *"You never let me visit my friends."* I did not think this was true. I could have said, *"That's not true. I always let you go."* (Posture versus posture.) Lots of conflict would probably have resulted, leading nowhere. Luckily, I put aside the trap for the moment and focused on the real issue. The real issue was whether my daughter could go out now. I agreed to consider the validity of her accusation but stated that today, I had to say no. The trick was to do this in a calm and relaxed way which did not respond to the posture of rebellion, anger, attack. I remained sympathetic to the accusation but maintained the wisdom of parental choice. I felt it was best to stay as distant as possible during our debate and this meant little eye contact and very little face-to-face discussion. After a while she too realized she needed the time at home and, I'm happy to say, she ended up thanking me.

UNIFYING POSTURES AND GESTURES

Whenever possible, it is better to have consistency between postures and gestures rather than risk misunderstanding. Consistent postures and gestures leave no ambiguity when our statement of intent is followed by appropriate action. The movements will be congruous in design and intensity when what we think we should do and what we actually do are compatible. Posture: *"We must take a tough stand against pollution."* Gesture: *"I am writing a check supporting this environmental group."*

One way to solve inconsistencies between postures and gestures is to recognize them and then find gestures which are consistent with our position. If we take the posture of an involved parent, we must find some way to act consistently with that statement. Otherwise we are paying lip service to the statement of involvement.

Receptive body posture: The body posture may be curved as if to create an inviting space to enter. It may relax, showing receptivity.

It could reach towards you, showing interest, or lower itself, allowing you to dominate for a time.

Conflicting gesture: The arms may move back to grasp the arms of the chair, or cross the body, or make a sign to stop. *"I want to be helpful,"* says the posture. But the gesture says, *"I had better reserve some part of me in case I need to get out of this."*

Find a statement which you can support with an action. Find a posture from which you can make a consistent gesture. You may not be able to go on a class trip, but instead can make costumes for the class play or coach the soccer team. Then the message becomes consistent.

When postures and gestures are not 'in sync' there may be good reasons. For example, college students, not yet sure about what they want to do, have a hard time making clear-cut statements about their future profession. They have to qualify their statements. They may feel uncomfortable and put on the spot. Their discomfort and indecisiveness may be more obvious in their postures and gestures than in their words. A professional, say, an engineer, who cannot find work is his chosen field, may find his postures and gestures contradict each other when he speaks about his work. Sometimes conflicts are not reconcilable. *"I love nature, but live in the city."* We live with these paradoxes until we can find solutions: a country house or summers away, for example.

We welcome some gestures that soften more pompous statuesque and inaccessible postures. If a person is authoritarian and rigid, in a domineering stance, she probably is demanding and unyielding. She dismisses people easily from this posture. She rarely relaxes her torso, there is little deviation of the head or spine, and she does not adapt her posture to anyone else's. A small, softening gesture would be very significant.

Often it can be a great relief to find a few inconsistent gestures. For instance, a young child in a pout or rage, peeks out at you when he thinks you are not looking to see what effect he is having. He is letting you know he is ready for a few conciliatory gestures. The gesture lets you know he is ready to let go of his posture, and you will soon be on the track toward a more workable relationship. How vital it is to recognize the posture being displayed. When we assume the appropriate posture, we show understanding and recognition for another person's need.

WHERE POSTURE AND GESTURE END
AND INTEGRATED MOVEMENT BEGINS

We have been looking at the way gestures and postures function. They reflect our thought process and regulate our communication. If we examine our gestures and postures we will gain a better grasp on the interlocking pieces of a relationship. Postures and gestures are the gears of the communication process which shift it and move it along.

However, these two important stylistic modes are inadequate to express creative, spontaneous, impulsive action; moments of total abandon. When we are carried away by our feelings, we are not concerned with details or formalities. Instead, everything is done from total conviction. For instance, when we are totally engrossed in the care of a baby, nothing else seems important. The intensity of these situations promotes an involvement which manifests physically as Integrated Movement.

Integrated Movement is smooth, continuous and complete. It follows a part of a spiral. It looks like a piece of a wave flowing around our body. We are totally absorbed by it. It might seem to float off lightly with humor or jest, or condense and press into the ground to reinforce a thought. This new entity born of posture and gesture emerges in its own right. It jumps the synapse between Posture and Gesture. For that moment who we are (posture) and what we are doing (gesture) are one.

We have left the safety of each of these options to risk being off balance, suspended, active, energized in a new way. Our movement is lending support and intensity to our thought which is seeking sincere and honest expression. We risk becoming ourselves.

Life-sized bronze sculpture titled, "Crack the Whip"

THREE

INTEGRATED MOVEMENT: THE MOMENT OF TRUTH

Integrated Movement is the expression of our involvement in what we are doing and saying.

> To discover Integrated Movement, speak to a friend with only gestures. It will be such a struggle to stay uninvolved that when you revert to normal, you will experience the Integrated Movement along with a huge sigh of relief!

DESCRIPTION OF INTEGRATED MOVEMENT

An Integrated Movement merges a posture and a gesture with a consistent quality, dynamic or shape. In an Integrated Movement, the same quality of movement has to travel through the posture and gesture. Therefore, if the hand turns and sweeps out to the side, the body has to do the same. If we search for something with our eyes, our body has to follow. It is this synthesis that is fully engaging. We are speaking and acting in a way that is fresh and new. We feel mobilized, energized, affirmed.

An Integrated Movement funnels into and out of a little body part, cycling between the periphery and the center of the body. It is compelling to an observer who can literally become transfixed for a moment by its power and energy.

We are not usually aware of body movement at all, but we can pay attention to gesture and we can bring it into awareness. We can also study posture and become aware of it. We must now focus on Integrated Movement and bring it too from the shadows into the light.

OBSERVING INTEGRATED MOVEMENT

When you decide to observe your own Integrated Movement, the decision itself will affect you. To observe Integrated Movement, you must *feel* what is happening as much as *see* it. You will find that your own thoughts and personal experiences will be submerged in the process of watching for this moment. As a result, you are becoming acutely sensitive and receptive to new worlds of information.

Observing animals, you can see an Integrated Movement in the leap of a squirrel, compared to the quick turns of its head from an immobile posture. The leap was an Integrated Movement and provided a bridge from the tree to the ground. Our Integrated Movements are also bridges, sometimes physical ones, as in a leap, a swing, a hoist.

Integrated Movement is automatically part of the things you do. It is in your walk, in the way you reach for an object on a shelf. When Integrated Movement is incorporated into your everyday actions or tasks, you will usually feel a sense of satisfaction in that task. (As a result, some people actually like to polish shoes or iron, while others enjoy reorganizing drawers or closets.) If an activity draws on your Integrated Movement preferences, you are likely to enjoy it. If not it will simply be a chore.

People have a particular way in which their Integrated Movement occurs among their gestures and postures. Some have long sequences of Integrated Movements and then none. In other people, Integrated Movements are sprinkled evenly along the course of their conversation or activity. Integrated Movement is very clear and obvious on some people and quite hidden on others. Some people can become aware of their Integrated Movement more easily than others. In some people Integrated Movements occur consistently throughout the day. In others they occur more sporadically.

COMMUNICATING WITH INTEGRATED MOVEMENT

Integrated Movement is most obvious in these seven situations:
1. Getting comfortable;
2. Affirming and confirming;
3. Being open;
4. Showing emotion;
5. Feeling needy;
6. Being expressive; and
7. Thinking creatively.

1. Getting comfortable

You are introduced to a new person. You settle down to be yourself and become familiar with the situation. Conversation begins and you are asked a question. As you gather your thoughts, you might pull on the lapels of your jacket and follow the movement through your body. You might tug on your skirt, or rearrange yourself in the chair with a full-body, consistent movement. These movements show that you are bringing yourself physically and mentally to the question. You are shedding your previous thoughts or activities and preparing for a new one. You are also aware that you will be dominating the picture for a bit, as the attention is now on you.

After each Integrated Movement a posture sets in. You pull yourself together with an Integrated movement as you prepare for the exchange or interaction which will follow. You then create the appropriate persona, or posture, to maintain the existing relationship. If you stay too long in a posture, you will become uncomfortable and distracted. Something in you triggers a change. If you wish to stay involved, you generate another Integrated Movement so that you remain present in the moment. Observe this by becoming aware of your own movements as you get comfortable in different situations.

2. Affirming and confirming

When you are in full agreement and believe whole-heartedly in what is being said, you show this physically. We often do an affirmative nod which reverberates through the whole body. The words *"you're right,"* or *"I agree,"* may accompany it and the speaker feels your support. You might confirm your pleasure at hearing good news by a little jump for joy. This kind of physical affirmation leaves little room for misunderstanding. It is a complete and satisfying communication. Even in cases when it is used to confirm a decision not to go ahead with a plan, it remains a complete communication. When it is used to reinforce discipline, it is satisfying because it shows no doubt or hesitation.

3. Being open

When you are sure that you will be received with proper attention and understanding, when your past experiences with similar situations have been positive, you will risk being open and fully share what you believe. While being open does not necessarily mean saying everything you want to say, it does mean feeling free to say what you believe in the best way you can. It may be the willingness to reveal something about yourself. It may be feeling open enough to say what you believe will be best for someone else. It means honestly owning up to what your heart feels. It is knowing what is in your mind and organizing it to be spoken effectively and honestly.

When no threats or dangers exist or when we are prepared to meet a danger, we use Integrated Movement. At those times we speak openly, without hesitation, qualification or artificiality. Openness in another person needs to be acknowledged. Unintentional rejection at these times can shut the doors on future honest communication.

4. Expressing emotion

You are filled with emotion and don't know why. Talking about it helps you identify the causes. Sharing it with someone comforts you. Experiencing emotions is a way to go from one phase of a situation to another. It is a source of energy which can be used creatively to solve a problem. It also can bring comfort and create closeness. Emotions are part of the limbic system of the old brain in the sense of our animal evolution. Experiences from this part of the brain are not accessible to the new brain, the neo-cortex, until they are recognized and expressed.

Expressing emotion can be scary. We sometimes feel it will overwhelm us or be inappropriate or be difficult to cope with in someone else. Failing to differentiate appropriate from inappropriate moments, we tend to hide emotions. Of course there are times when emotional displays are unacceptable, but in the proper context they are the very essence of our humanness.

5. Feeling needy

Awareness of personal feelings and emotions are the signals which identify need. Making a bridge between emotion and need gives us a way to solve a problem. *"I need more time to finish this job." "I need more help." "I need more sympathy."* When we ask for our needs directly, we make it easier for others to satisfy them. When we make it a puzzle to be solved, not everyone wants to play the game.

Putting your needs into an Integrated Movement statement, one which says and shows what you mean, carries its own satisfaction. It means you have taken a vague, amorphous discomfort and resolved it, distilled it to a specific need. You can now focus on its fulfillment, or even deal with its absence. The frustration is greatly reduced. It means you are no longer going to be more attached to the state of neediness than to the solution. *"I would like you to speak quietly even when you are angry." "I would like you to hug me when I am crying."* The guesswork is gone. Be patient. The response may not be immediate, but it is on its way.

In another example, something is bothering you and you need to express it. You thought you could put it aside, but it returns with a vengeance. You need to discover why. Perhaps you are afraid you will not get what you want. (You may not. In that case, you may have to provide what you need yourself.) Or you might be afraid that if your need is satisfied, it will not be what you thought it was. (You are always free to make new adjustments.) If in fact you will not be satisfied with any solution, then at least you can stop blaming others and accept your circumstances honestly.

6. Being expressive

You might want to describe the beauty of a sunset you vividly remember. Your body responds to the memory, changing subtly to reflect the feelings you had. When you talk about an experience like this, you become absorbed, and Integrated Movement dominates the postures and gestures. You become involved in recreating or reexperiencing the feelings you felt before. Your full participation indicates the importance you wish to give the event. When something has moved you and you can fully express the experience to someone else, you feel complete. New connections are made. New relevance. New meaning. The expression is its own goal.

7. Thinking creatively

You have struggled with an idea. Suddenly you are generating new thoughts. The possibilities are there. You are fully engaged. You are mentally trying things, experimenting. Your body is fully energized. Whether in a business deal, decorating, or writing a book, creative inspiration is totally engaging. Moments of insight release a flow of energy which becomes an Integrated Movement. Something is understood or a new plan is made.

When people feel comfortable in a team, communication flows easily. Individual ideas or concerns are respected. The signals for speaking and listening are natural. People feel good as a result of full, active participation. Observing movement when listening lets you really hear what the other person is saying. Creative decisions get made. Things get accomplished.

Creative moments can't be forced, but certain conditions have been found to be more conducive than others: respect and support, meditation and relaxation, emergencies, humor, friendliness.

When you use the concept of Integrated Movement to improve a relationship or a communication, you are doing one or more of the following things:

1. Expressing something new;
2. Being as honest as possible;
3. Being as effective as possible;
4. Revealing your inner self and accepting the consequences;
5. Being open to the possibility of rejection;
6. Being open to acceptance;
7. Inviting the possibility of change;
8. Being the center of attention;

9.   Finding out more than you knew before; and

10.   Being without artifices of gesture and posture.

When you see Integrated Movement in someone, you are responding to the commitment they have expressed. You are acknowledging them in a most important way. This will affect your relationship. By becoming aware of Integrated Movement you are taking responsibility for your communication. You are identifying and expressing your needs eloquently.

As we search for what would integrate us we learn to present ourselves and our ideas optimally. Sometimes we are so caught in feeling blocked or blaming others that we don't see solutions which already exist. Attention to Integrated Movement prods us to use our emotions, feelings and thoughts as we communicate.

TRYING IT OUT

It is time for you to feel your own Integrated Movement within yourself.

1.   Practice a movement which starts in your foot and continues forward until your whole body has followed. That is an Integrated Movement. Turn your head to look at something and before you stop, feel the rest of your body support the looking.

That is an Integrated Movement. Settle back into your chair and consider the importance of what you have just experienced.. You have now felt the physical quality of an Integrated Movement.

2.   To experience the accompanying state of mind, close your eyes. This helps you shut out distractions and focus on the internal process of movement. Review the posture you are in. Trace it in your mind's eye. Feel the nature of it. Decide what it is, i.e., you are leaning back against a tree, your arms are folded and your legs stretched out.

You are relaxed, inward, and slightly withdrawn from action, in a more meditative attitude. You remember something really important that you have to do.

Make the changes your body wants to make to get ready to do this. Feel the way you pull yourself together and reorganize into a new posture. This is an Integrated Movement getting you ready for a new task, a new state of mind.

3.   Try another approach to feeling your Integrated Movement. Feel your starting posture. Think of something you want to tell a close friend about an important break-through you made.

With your eyes open or closed, say the words to yourself. Did you feel your body change? That was an Integrated Movement.

I asked you to say the words to yourself so that you would feel the movement and not forget to observe yourself. Now try the same movement and accompany it with the same words.

Open your eyes and say the words aloud. This will give you practice feeling Integrated Movement while you are speaking. ❖

Take some time every day to observe yourself. You can do it after dinner, during lunch or even while talking to a friend on the telephone. Divide everything you do, every movement, into the categories of posture, gesture and Integrated Movement. Fixing breakfast will provide you with lots of gestural movements. If you do any warm-up or exercise, it is likely to have all three movements in it. This is, of course, one reason why you feel good, more alert, when you are done. (See chapter 9.)

For example, if you scold someone, even a pet, using just your head and hand, that is a gesture. If you feel really indignant and plant your feet and look menacing, that is a posture. If you bend down getting ready to say with meaning, *"that is not acceptable,"* you are using an Integrated Movement. Do you sense the difference? Good.

After you have watched yourself for a while and tried to differentiate postures from gestures and from Integrated Movement, you may have questions.

Here are some guidelines. Bear in mind that there are movements which remain difficult to define.

Question: *How can I tell the difference between lots of gestures and an Integrated Movement?*

Answer: In a movement where a hand goes one way, the head another way, there is no consistency and no Integrated Movement. If one body part is quick and sharp and another is curved and limp, it is not an Integrated Movement. You have many things to do, and no one thing is totally absorbing you. Instead you are trying to do them all at once. The body looks very busy. This happens when your thoughts are in a million places at once. Mothers are familiar with this: cooking, watching a crawling child, and talking on the telephone. Executives are familiar with this: one call on one phone, another one ringing; someone waiting for instructions; the secretary signaling that a client has arrived. This is high animation and needs many gestures to keep everything in action. Again, overlapping gestures are inconsistent. They bear no relationship to each other.

Question: *How can I distinguish large postures from Integrated Movements?*

Answer: A posture does not flow. An Integrated Movement does. A posture is static. An Integrated Movement leads you on. A posture will feel like the body is held in a block. It has been lifted and lowered, pushed or pulled. It is more like a display or joke, an imitation. It does not lead anywhere. A therapeutic posture will let your muscles stretch so that when you relax your body feels revitalized. If your body has been holding an attentive posture, listening to a long story, you might feel the discomfort and stretch your spine like a cat. You might rub your neck, extend your legs and arch your back all at the same time. This is a posture. All parts are not flowing together. You are breaking out of a mold, not yet developing a new thought. A posture can also be a continuous movement which never breaks into a gesture, like rocking.

Question : *What does an Integrated Movement really feel like?*

Answer: It feels like a magnetic field which you are energizing with your movement. It feels like a teacher who is having a wonderful time sharing her experience and interests and enjoying being the center of attention. It feels like a perfect golf swing; your first success riding a bicycle; a graceful swan dive, hitting a home run. It feels like a flow of movement between the body and a limb. It is a flow between the self and the environment.

The phrase *Integrated Movement* was specifically chosen to refer to the way a posture and gesture blend, merge into one movement. It is the integration of thought and action as the body expresses the mind. Keep looking for moments when you feel the shift into an Integrated Movement. Don't worry about mistakes. You will eventually become familiar with the way your thoughts change, the way your body feels and you will know. Then, you will be synthesizing your feelings and needs, thinking them through creatively, making yourself comfortable as you express them with the whole body commitment they deserve.

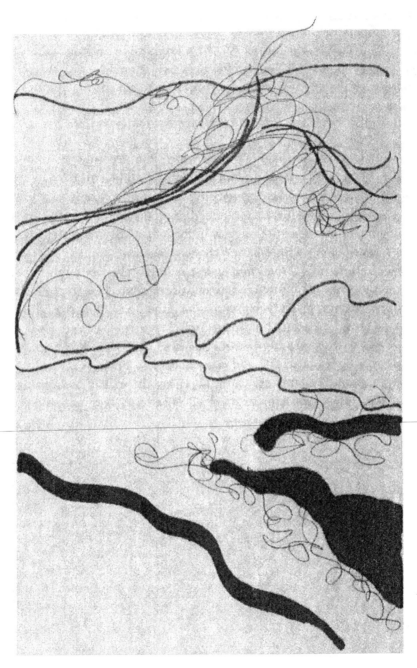

Jocelyn Berry, "Waves"

FOUR

EXPERIENCING
INTEGRATED MOVEMENT

VISUALIZATION EXERCISE

1.   Close your eyes. Picture yourself standing in the ocean as a smooth wave comes rolling in.

2.   Give a little push with your feet; the wave lifts you up and lowers you down. That is the feeling of Integrated Movement.

3.   Now, lift your right arm and let an imaginary wave take the rest of your body with it. As the wave passes, feel your body lower and your arm follow. The movement is smooth. There is no sense of separateness at the joint or anywhere else. There is no pause between the arm and the body movement.

4.   You are being lifted, but you are not consciously doing anything. It feels more like something is happening to you. And it is. There is a feeling of letting go to the movement. (You can also think of it as a ray of light or a sound vibration traveling through you).

The physical sense of letting go also characterizes the psychological feeling: letting go of the statement, the idea, the thought.

You are:

❖ letting go of constraint, formality, inhibition;

❖ letting go of being told what to do and how to do it;

❖ letting go to a feeling inside that wants expression.

The exact words come riding along with the feeling. They come spontaneously and eloquently.

Building on this:

---

1. Repeat the movement experience of riding the wave, and this time describe aloud how it feels.

    "I feel buoyant and free."

    "I feel supported in my upper back."

    "I feel like a child playing."

    "I feel scared of getting lost in the unknown, or in the power of the wave."

2. Now take a pencil and make a spontaneous drawing of your movement. You don't have to plan what you are going to do ahead of time. Be free. The drawing itself is not important; capturing the feeling on paper is important. Look at your drawing for any information it can provide about your Integrated Movement.

3. Make another drawing. This time let your body move the pencil. Feel the connection between your arm and the rest of your body. This is an Integrated Movement and the drawing is the trace form of your movement.

Finding an Integrated Movement is a discipline of the mind as well as the body. You have already formed thinking habits of posture and gesture which may have outlived their usefulness. These can get in the way when you want to be creative or discover change. In youth, spontaneity and creativity abound. With age, however, these become qualities to fight for. You must continue to revise and recreate yourself throughout your life. Integrated Movement keeps you alive to the moment.

INTEGRATED MOVEMENT THROUGH THE MIND'S EYE

1. As we are rarely empty of secondary thoughts, find the kernel of a thought that is in your mind now. Stop reading for a moment and write it down. The secondary thought gets in the way of a full expression of Integrated Movement. Writing it down allows us to clear it from mind. Now we are ready for a less immediate but perhaps larger thought.

2. Now pause again and think about what you would like to learn from this book. How will it help you accomplish something important to you? Tell this thought to a friend as a way of experiencing your Integrated Movement.

3. As you tell it, feel the change in your body. Feel the way your interest intensifies. Feel the way your body seems to gather in support of your thought. Is there a wave-like feeling that seems to move through you? If your answer is yes, you have successfully created an Integrated Movement by paying close attention to your thoughts.

4. Give your friend an opportunity to participate. Ask a leading question, i.e., What do you need most in your life now? What would you most like to do? What is the most interesting thing you are working on?

5. Make sure to watch your partner from the very minute you ask the question. Do you see any change? (It may precede the answer or occur during her response.) Did you see an increase in intensity or involvement which flowed through the whole body? If so, you have observed an Integrated Movement.

To recognize the development of an Integrated Movement ask yourself:
- ❖ Did I lead up to an Integrated Movement, shifting, posturing and gesturing until I became absorbed?
- ❖ Did I go right to the heart of the idea with an Integrated Movement?

❖   Did I fail to notice my Integrated Movement because I was so
involved in the topic?

With this new sensitivity you can choose to reduce frivolous or unimportant
discussions in favor of personally significant and interesting issues. Enjoy the
richness of communication which follows.

Integrated Movement Approached Through Physical Skill And Coordination: The Bean Bag Toss

This is an exercise for a group.

1.   Gesture: Stand close together. Toss the bean bag and catch it from
the elbow. Take a few turns so you can really feel the sense of
gesture in the action.

2.   Posture: Now toss it as if it were an awkward object; a pillow that is
falling apart, a long branch. Use your whole body in a block,
throwing it as one piece. Watch each participant as you do this
in order to make mental note of the body involvement in this
activity.

3.   Integrated Movement: With more space between you, if necessary,
throw your object with concentration on getting it right to your
goal. Make a smooth arc. Feel the preparation, the moment of action. Prolong it and the follow-through. Let the gesture of the
arm lead through the whole body. Catch the same way. Accommodate your shape to the object. Cushion yourself from a
pretend impact.

4.   As you catch the bean bag, exaggerate the movement so that you
can clearly feel the arm catching and the body accommodating.
Extend the moment of connection by slowing it down. (Connect
the catch smoothly into the throw for another moment of Integrated Movement).

How does each movement feel to you? Which feels the best? Which looks the most skilled and professional? (Of course there were times when an Integrated Movement for a small toss would look very inappropriate.)

Looking at physical activity for examples of Integrated Movement is good training. Watch frisbee players and the beautiful connected movements that often accompany a throw or a catch. We are accustomed to observing the skill and grace of Integrated Movement in sports. We can do this in daily life as well.

An Integrated Movement Can Start from a Posture or a Gesture

1. The alarm clock rings. You sit up suddenly from a deep sleep, (posture). You turn off the alarm clock and luxuriously sink back into your pillow for an extra ten minutes (Integrated Movement).

2. Look around for your missing keys with exasperation (gestures), and then spot them on the counter. The transition between the recognition and the action of getting them is the Integrated Movement.

3. Imagine you are entering the water prepared to throw yourself in and expecting it to be cold. Instead, the water is warm and comfortable. The tension releases as you submerge yourself and start to swim. That is the Integrated Movement. Your body has prepared with a posture and given way to an Integrated Movement.

A gesture becoming an Integrated Movement might happen like this: Imagine offering someone a helping hand. You extend your hand gradually, letting your body follow. The message is: *"May I help you?"* The recipient says *"yes,"* as she takes your hand and leaps over a puddle, supported by your pull. For that short moment, the relationship involved support. She let go to her Integrated Movement. Your gesture signaled your readiness to get involved.

If you always have a comfortable gesture ready, you may find it easy to enter and exit situations. With gestures, you may start out at a distance and then gradually become involved. With posture, you are immediately involved. Observe some of your personal exchanges. Do you need an invitation to participate in a group? Can you present yourself to a new crowd with no introductions?

Of course certain situations demand certain behavior, but we still have our preferences. Discover yours.

MIRRORING INTEGRATED MOVEMENT

Our responsiveness to other people's movement is usually limited to unconscious mirroring of postures, or rhythmic patterns in gestures. In this exercise you and your partner will exaggerate the mirroring process.

To Ponder:

1. Designate a leader.
2. The leader begins to make deliberate and slow-motion movements allowing one body part to start and gradually lets the rest of the body follow through. Then the leader deliberately ends the movement.
3. Partner mirrors the movement.
4. The leader varies the size, shape and quality of her movement as the partner continues to mirror. (Leader, explore your repertory of movement until you and your partner are totally comfortable with the phrasing and flow of movement.)
5. Now, exchange leadership.

❖ Did the mirroring become comfortable?
❖ Did you lose the sense of who was leading?
❖ Did you find a comfortable breathing pattern?
❖ Did your movements become synchronized?

Question: *Should we do everyday movements, like picking things up from the floor, or more abstract movement?*

Answer: Either is fine. You may want to start with everyday movement and allow it to become more abstract.

Question: *I am having a hard time following my partner. What should I do?*

Answer: Ask her to be sure her gestures are clear, and that the movement carries through the whole body. The leader should be sure to make clear beginnings and endings so that the partner can follow easily.

At first you may find it hard to watch and move at the same time. Don't think about learning the movement, just empathize and follow. The movement does not have to be perfect. You do not have to start on the same foot!

Think of following a musical scale. Feel where your body wants to go next. Let the movement have its own logic. Follow the movement with your voice, then you have an auditory mirror as well. Feel connected to your partner by invisible threads. Keep breathing and relaxing. Let the body think for itself. If it is still difficult, shift leadership. After you have experienced leading, you may find it easier to follow.

Question: *I can't feel when the Integrated Movement happens.*

Answer: Leader, emphasize the transitions. Sing the melody of your movement. Feel it crescendo and decrescendo. 'Hear' the moment of emphasis. Make specific energetic gestures, then follow through into a total body action. Change levels to encourage whole-body involvement. Use turns, or locomotion.[1]

MIRRORING EVERYDAY MOVEMENT

Some movements feel like exertions and some feel like recuperations. Some expend energy, some replace it. By now you are becoming attuned to easily identifying Integrated Movement.

---

1. Leader, you might start the movement by pressing your arm into the arm of your chair, (gesture). Both leader and follower, notice where the movement starts and stops.

2. Do it once again. Let the movement of pressing travel down the side of your body into your feet until you feel the strain of pressing your whole body into the chair and floor. This is an exaggerated Integrated Movement while sitting.

3. Now start the movement from your feet, until you feel it in your arm.

4. Make the movements in slow motion so that your partner can follow easily.

5. Highlight the moment when the movement comes together.

APPLYING VIDEO TECHNOLOGY TO MOVEMENT ANALYSIS

Videotape is a powerful tool for observing movement. Use it to study yourself and get feedback from others. Concentrate on your movement. Don't be distracted by how you look.

---

1. Videotape two or three people in conversation for ten to fifteen minutes.

2. When you review the tape, look for movements that carry through the whole body. In case of doubt, the person who was moving can verify the Integrated Movement, since she will remember her involvement.

3. Each person should mimic her own gestures to become familiar with the feeling and expression of them.

   You may be self-conscious or distracted if you have many more gestures than you thought. (Most people think they don't move.) However, you can easily turn the self-consciousness into self-awareness.

4. Each person mirrors her own posture, and discusses its quality and statement.

To Ponder:

- ❖ Did you have more gestures than you thought?
- ❖ Was it easier to observe without participating in the conversation?
- ❖ Did you see things in people you know well that you hadn't noticed before?
- ❖ Some people feel a bonding as a result of observing each other's Integrated Movement. Did this happen to you?

You have experienced Integrated Movement now in several ways: through imagining, feeling, exaggerating; by leading movement and following it; and by observing video. This is the necessary groundwork so that your body will now know the experience of Integrated Movement when it happens in the customary conversational way.

Now for a shift of focus. The next exercise will heighten your involvement in a way that will allow an Integrated Movement to happen naturally and give you the chance to pinpoint it.

1. Think of someone you really admire: perhaps an athlete, a rock star, a dancer, or a tennis pro.

2. Talk to a friend about how great you think the celebrity is. Get carried away!

3. Concentrate on a moment when you are transported into the movement. (Integrated Movement)

4. Feel your own sense of enthusiasm when you talk about the person's skill. Are you clear about the moment of Integrated Movement? Is it easier to feel when talking about someone else?

5. Now, take this good, nourishing feeling you have when you describe the person you admire and talk about something you care about in your own life. Do this until you have experienced at least one Integrated Movement on your own project, goal, vision, dream.

6. Discuss the moments which felt the most Integrated to you and see if your partner agrees. Come to agreement based on the physical feeling, the speaker's enthusiasm and the listener's involvement.

Individual reactions vary and are equally valid:

"When I was personally involved in the topic, I started using lots of Integrated Movements. I also thought of myself as initiating moments of 'truth'."

"I feel there is Integrated Movement when there is action."

"You may need to make some people angry to see Integrated Movement, otherwise, they keep a polite, infuriating distance."

"It was like a fire building in intensity. I started Integrating and I didn't want to stop."

"I felt lost in my own world."

"When I lost my fear and just spoke from my own experience, I became Integrated."

"As I practiced, I found that abstract concepts inhibited my Integrated Movement."

"I feel I do this same kind of listening and encouraging in my counseling work. It is good to be able to analyze it from a movement point of view."

"Although I was not very interested in the conversation at first, when I began to see Integrated Movement, I started to feel I was opening up."

"It seems to me that if Integrated Movement takes place, it is coupled with a desire to communicate. It is reaching out. It is a sign of healthy involvement."

SIGNALING INTEGRATED MOVEMENT IN NATURAL BEHAVIOR

This exercise is designed to help you become familiar with your own Integrated Movement so that you can call on it to generate breakthrough ideas at will and support others to do the same. (See pp. 50, 51.) Signalling gives the speaker valuable feedback that an Integrated Movement is happening now and gives the listener practice in identifying and supporting Integrated Movement. The listener will mark the moment of Integrated Movement for the speaker. Give yourself a good 15 minutes for this exercise so that you can really discuss the topic in depth.

1. Talk about your most successful experience, something you are proud of either in your career or in your personal life. Be descriptive. Speaker: *"I am proud of my daughter."* Listener: *"Why? What has she done that you are proud of?"*

2. As you talk, your partner will watch the large and small movements that convey your sincerity. The listener will see, feel and hear these moments best by being relaxed and receptive. The listener must keep circling the speaker's body with his eyes and feel when he is drawn in to the speaker's experience.

3. Speaker: when you feel a movement go through your whole body, stop and say, *"now,"* or *"that was one."* Then go on. You will be helping the listener. She has a difficult task, being fully engrossed in your conversation and being alert to your movements.

4. When you experience an Integrated Movement, you should ask yourself, *"What was I saying at that moment? What meaning did it have for me?"*

5. Gradually the listener will take over making the signal for you so that you don't have to stop and point it out.

6. Listener: you need to find a gesture that suits you, to identify the Integrated Movement. Try to find a signal which does not disrupt the flow of conversation.

You can vary this exercise by having a third person participate whose sole responsibility will be to signal Integrated Movement.

GUIDELINES FOR THE LISTENER

❖ Trace the outline of the mover with your eyes, in a subtle way, keeping a sense of the whole.

❖ Follow the mover's movement in a very small way in your body.

❖ Do not TRY to see. Relax and breathe. Let your eyes rest. Feel them as two pools of calm water.[2] Do not reach for observations.

❖ If you feel yourself getting tired during this exercise, rest and return to a sense of your own breath. Rest your eyes by looking into the distance. Remember it is your whole body that is seeing, not just your eyes.

FOR THE SPEAKER

- ❖ The speaker may choose to totally ignore the signals. If so, this is an indication of her need to participate fully in the communication.
- ❖ If the speaker is too distracted by the signal, one remedy is for the signaler to stop until the speaker is more engrossed in the conversation.

Another remedy is to try another kind of signal: a 'yes' or an 'uh hum' with some emphasis.

- ❖ The speaker might try signaling his own Integrated Movements.

The goal is to be able to sense our own Integrated Movement and the accompanying thought without assistance.

Take time to process your experience. If you felt scared or uncomfortable in this exercise, don't judge yourself. Just make note of your reaction. The most valuable knowledge to be gained from the exercise is knowing your own patterns of communication. If you have learned more about yourself, you have succeeded.

THE NEXT STEP: THE LISTENER'S REACTIONS

What happens when you see a variety of responses to Integrated Movement? How does it affect the Integrated Movement? Here are three experiences to compare and discuss. If you decide to wait until you have changed roles before talking it over, then the first person should make careful notes of her observations.

A FREEZE RESPONSE

> When you see your partner's Integrated Movement, freeze. Do not move. Resume moving when the Integrated Movement is over.

This response made some people reduce the intensity of their communication, change the subject or invite the listener to speak. Others created an imaginary, sympathetic listener. The need for communication intensified. Their Integrated Movements got bigger and bigger, as if shouting to be heard.

A GESTURE RESPONSE

> Next, respond to the speaker with a gesture when you see an
> Integrated Movement.

Some people felt that because they had taken a risk and given trust, they
wanted more than a gesture in response. Others felt rejected. For some, a
gesture in response was all they needed.

INTEGRATED MOVEMENT RESPONSE

> Now respond to your partner's Integrated Movement with one of
> your own. Either match the feeling and mood of the Integrated
> Movement you saw, giving appropriate verbal support, or respond in
> a way that is comfortable to you, where you sincerely share your con-
> cern, agreement, approval in a demonstrative way.

Most people found that the Integrated Movement response was the most
satisfying. They felt heard and understood. Fewer people found an attentive
posture satisfactory, but under no circumstances was a frozen response acceptable.

It is possible to be overwhelmed by Integrated Movement when it is too
intense and emotional. Our usual response is to fidget, turn away, give uncomfortable signals which often intensifies the speaker's efforts. This response
encourages intensity.

To test this, go back to our last exercise and ask your listener to fidget, make
no eye contact, express impatience or annoyance while you talk about something
emotional.

To experience the contrast, ask your listener to respond in a big way, with
a large movement of his/her body, to match the size and intensity of your
Integrated Movement. What response helped you most, a big movement or
gestures of discomfort? Subtle cues do not work if someone is used to taking and

holding the spotlight, is enthralled with the topic, is out of control and can't stop even though you are not listening. A large movement is usually necessary.

Pamela and I tried to sense the tiniest change in our own bodies which be responsible for change in a listener's experience.

Pam: *"While you were talking, I sat thinking 'how boring this is. It doesn't interest me at all.' Then the next time, I was seeking to understand what you were saying. My body felt very different, though the change was subtle. At first, my cells felt closed. The surface of my skin was a boundary. I was not letting myself be affected by what you were saying. The thought in my mind created a very subtle negative posture which did not let you in."*

Ellen: *"The first time, you seemed encased in a block of ice. The second time you seemed alive."*

We reversed roles. I made my shifts in thought and Pam easily guessed which were hostile and which receptive. We can easily tell, if we pay attention, when someone is withholding a response to our Integrated Movement expression. The eyes harden and become still. The surface tension of the body changes. When receptive, the eyes seem to follow the movement, as if caressing the shape of the speaker.

Without any large shifts of posture or gesture, we can clearly get our message across. Listening from a purely meditative state makes understanding easy. Creative options appear.

FOCUS ON A PROBLEM AND GENERATE AN INTEGRATED MOVEMENT

You are annoyed and frustrated by a colleague who is monopolizing a conversation and making you late. If you argue, it will only prolong the debate. If you say nothing and leave, it remains unresolved. What will take you beyond the frustration? Think fast. Be polite and sincere. *"Sally, I have to interrupt. We only have ten minutes left and we need a solution before we end the meeting."* Support your statement with an Integrated Movement equal in size and intensity to Sally's, even if you have to stand up. Make direct eye contact.

Recap:

- ❖ Recognize a personal or group need.
- ❖ Formulate an approach to resolve the difficulty for this moment. Note your thought to yourself or on paper.
- ❖ Wait a bit to confirm the need for your solution.
- ❖ Find or create an appropriate moment to speak.
- ❖ Begin to feel a wave-like quality through your body. Trust it. Go with it. Let the thought take form and speak.
- ❖ End your statement as the Integrated Movement ebbs away.

Finding a statement that lets you feel whole, puts you in the frame of mind for honestly stating your need. You can at the very least state that you want a solution. You want to get past the frustration and into understanding. Your openness to the solution will allow for one.

INTEGRATED MOVEMENT AS SELF-DISCOVERY

Integrated Movement is an enormously helpful tool for use in breaking down your own rigid views and replacing them with fuller understanding.

1. Discuss a topic on which you have held rigid views. Example: Although I consider myself liberal, I am against the use of marijuana, even by adults. (This is the acknowledged posture.)

2. Your partner will challenge your views in order to understand your position more deeply.

3. Defend your viewpoint until your own conversation reveals a moment when you express a new rationale. This refreshing and totally satisfying moment, the Integrated Movement, is the discovery of new insight. Your body actually changes. It might expand its shape and slow down in energy, accompanying the statement: i.e., *"What bothers me is that people use drugs instead of developing other personal resources which will benefit them more."*

The following is an example of using Integrated Movement to solve problems:

"My friend and I were discussing how blocked she was about completing her Masters thesis. She was ready to give up. As the conversation began, all I heard were problems and all I saw were gestures. I challenged her position. Then, with full body involvement, she said: 'My biggest fear is that I will try to do my best and it won't be good enough.' This revelation was so meaningful that we both were transfixed for a few moments, realizing that this was the key to getting back to work. Next, we established a work schedule and agreed upon a verbal support system. She was filled with new enthusiasm."

FREQUENT QUESTIONS ABOUT INTEGRATED MOVEMENT

Question: *Does Integrated Movement always feel natural, deep and meaningful?*

Answer: Some people are timid with Integrated Movement. They do find it natural but may find it hard to do or to see on others.

Question: *Are there circumstances where Integrated Movement is out of place?*

Answer: Yes. For instance, if a politician asks us questions about our personal life, we think it's odd. However, we would like to see Integrated Movement when he talks about his commitment to issues and policy. It might be out of place at a formal dinner to discuss problems working with your boss in an intense, integrated way when your dinner companions are only acquaintances. Yet it is nice at a party to find someone you can really talk to about topics of substance.

Question: *Can Integrated Movement ever be abrupt rather than free-flowing?*

Answer: It can look abrupt, but not mechanical.

Question: *Can Integrated Movement be faked?*

Answer: Here is the answer I once gave in a workshop:
"To answer your question, watch my postures, gestures and Integrated Movements. You be the judge. 'No, it can't be faked,' I said, using a posture and gesture but no Integrated Movement. Why would one want to? Then again, it could be of advantage to manipulate people in this way. (I am still searching for a meaningful answer.) I want people to be so good at perceiving the true

nature of Integrated Movement that no one could be fooled. I want to solve communication problems, not create them! (That statement was said with Integrated Movement.) Dancers and actors practice recreating exact movement, yet they are still not 'faking.' They use memories, imagery and internal experiences to make it spontaneous and alive. We can do the same, (explaining with gestures)."

Question: *Can we hide our true feelings behind an Integrated Movement?*

Answer: No, the body will have some way to leak the truth. Some part of your body will reveal the fact that the investment is not fully there, that you have doubts.

Question: *How can I best use this material?*

Answer: First of all, by focusing on your needs and stating them with an Integrated Movement you can draw yourself out of a state of confusion and into clarity. This is a skill for everyone. Why hope that someone will guess what is on your mind? Being unclear is risky. You must avoid any conflicting, ambivalent concerns. Integrated Movement practice helps you do this.

Second, you can present yourself to others confidently, although you may have doubts or insecurities. Your performance at important interviews and presentations often benefits from practice and rehearsal. List the difficult questions you anticipate. Role-play them until you have satisfactory answers as demonstrated by Integrated Movement. In the process, you may discover fears, disguised in postures, which will hold you back. You may discover inappropriate gestures which diminish the power of your statements. Keep going until you can be confident of your performance.

Third, your awareness of Integrated Movement can help you maintain involvement and initiative in your work environment. Imagine that a valued employee comes to you with a suggestion you have to reject, but you want to be sure the employee does not withdraw his creative contribution to the job. You have to match his level of investment with your Integrated Movement to be truly convincing about how much you value him as an employee. You cannot give a quick 'no', to his suggestion and expect him not to be offended.

Fourth, you can use Integrated Movement to generate real commitment to a task. As you show your real enthusiasm, you will help clear away the doubts and hesitation of your colleagues.

Movement. You say, *"The way you said that makes me think there is more to it."* Probably there is. Your awareness of the movement keeps you from interpreting the event as offensive or hostile. It helps you through the little skirmishes of friendship.

Sixth, you can avoid awkward situations. Over lunch you begin talking with a colleague about ways to improve the organization of the office. You enjoy a nice rapport and are finally taking the opportunity to express these thoughts. You begin to talk freely and sense your involvement, trusting that you have an attentive listener. Just as you are really getting started, your colleague calls for the check. You sense your time is up. You can:

❖ React as if a door were slammed in your face;

❖ Ignore it and keep speaking, exasperating your colleague;

❖ Get a pencil and jot your thoughts down so that you don't forget them;

❖ Ask if your colleague is interested in continuing this discussion at another time; or

❖ Decide this is a good beginning and talk to someone else to solve the problem.

The first and second are the common responses. The rest give you more options and help you retain your creativity.

Take a deep breath, dear Reader. You have reached a high point in the study of movement. You have experienced Integrated Movement deliberately, physically, intellectually and emotionally. You have felt it in conversation and you have seen it in others. You know the discomfort associated with different responses to it. You have made personal discoveries and solved problems through your knowledge of Integrated Movement.

You now have an idea of the scope and importance of posture and gesture and Integrated Movement, the three essential elements in the art of communication. As we continue, you will see how that knowledge can be applied in the context of family, friends and relationships.

FIVE

FRIENDSHIP

If you were asked to describe what you like about a friend, would you mention movement? Probably not. Trust, comfort, common interests, understanding, yes. But we know that all these qualities are expressed in movement. Movement adds magnetism to your words. Yet this fragile quality can disappear easily. If friends can just maintain the level of expression and responsiveness that is the strength of their bond, the friendship will last a lifetime.

THE DEVELOPMENT OF FRIENDSHIP

Friendship is the ability to come together in a dependable flow of openness. When you are with a good friend you do not have to select or judge your Integrated Movement. You can turn on the faucet and let it all pour out. You trust that your friend can cope with the intensity. You trust your signals, you don't edit or revise. You trust the thoughts and images that flow between you. More is said with fewer words and a high context of understanding builds.[1] You create thoughts and ideas while you are expressing them. Enthusiasm ignites you both. Insights flow easily into each other's worlds.

An encounter moves toward a friendship when bonds are established. The usual stages in a developing friendship are:

Gestures 'break the ice,' postures create rapport, Integrated Movement establishes trust and respect.

Patterns of friendship can crop up almost anywhere: at the local fish market you exchange a few friendly words with a clerk; the merchant remembers your last order. The next thing you know, you have a sense of belonging and loyalty. Now, it's no longer "the" fish market, but "my" fish market. Regular patterns become rituals. We depend on them for a sense of community. We miss them when they change.

Apartment living in particular allows for many gesture-style communications. Interactions with neighbors can carry over through many years, and one feels sad every time a familiar family moves. Although these relationships are meaningful, in most cases, a respectful distance is maintained.

The next time you meet a new neighbor, become conscious of the body movement you see. These six pointers will help:

1. How many gestures where there?
2. Did the conversation feel comfortable or awkward?
3. Were conditions of status or dominance established? How?
4. Were overtures made to move beyond gestures?
5. Did the gestures establish points of common interest, both in topic and rhythm?
6. How did the encounter end?

Think about your conversation. If you found points of common interest, you may have the makings of a friendship. Perhaps you are both in the midst of building summer houses. You probably felt a sense of rapport, seen in shared postures and an occasional Integrated Movement. This is usually the extent of a pleasant exchange. Both people will feel good about it. Nothing further will happen until circumstances bring you together again, or one of you steps forward, risks rejection, and invites the other into deeper contact or communication.

There are some people you see infrequently. You visit, have tea, talk about the garden or local politics. Each time a little more is shared, more stories are exchanged, more personal details revealed. As you feel less like an intruder your reserved posture gives way. You have knitted a pattern which begins to integrate automatically. A deeper concern permeates the communication and hugs and kisses are shared in meeting and parting. Can you remember a situation where you felt this shift from a casual friendship? Initially, you may have attributed it to word-content alone. Now try to remember the physical change that happened. This was the turning point.

Then we all have a sprinkling of friendships of operatic intensity, people whose lives we follow in minute detail. We keep tightly bonded to the stories and outcomes of individual decisions. We respond to our friends' successes and failures as if they were our own.

When close friends trust each other enough to talk about themselves freely they no longer resort to postures and role-playing. They are not impressing each other with a resume of accomplishments and skills but are comfortable enough to reveal insecurities and emotional need. Presenting yourself in a less-than-perfect light is a stage in the development of friendship.

To get to this stage, someone must take a chance. Jane did by talking about her plans in an unedited, free flow of her feelings. She was struggling to describe her goals for a research project. I asked her to tell me the best outcome she could imagine. Everything she said sounded like postures. I encouraged her to go further: "What would you love to know or find out from this study?" Now I noticed big postural shifts as Jane searched for new ideas. Finally, with an Integrated Movement, she expressed her idealistic and practical vision for her study on education.

Movement is integral to every stage of a friendship. Movement monitors disagreements and reunions. Conscious use of movement is a way of taking conscious control. Using a simple, clear gesture reduces accidental expression of secondary emotions, personal need, discomfort when all that is asked of the situation is a statement of the facts at the moment.[2]

Take a few moments to practice choosing the right gesture and matching words to relieve internal tension. Many levels of honesty exist in our own intra-psychic processes.

1. Recognize your needs;

2. Find polite words;

3. Let your body use its comfortable, familiar gesture. (If you have used an Integrated Movement accidentally, it just means that your feelings were stronger than you thought.

Thinking about the mechanics of how to do this actually takes longer than doing it.

ANALYZING COMMUNICATION BY LOOKING AT MOVEMENT

Setting:	A New York City rent-controlled upper West Side apartment
Participants:	Kathy, from Australia
	Penny, from London, England
	Evelyn, the New York hostess
Situation:	Penny is Evelyn's house guest. Kathy arrives to visit her friend, Penny.

Analysis Between Evelyn and Penny:

Evelyn: *"When your good friend Kathy started talking, I saw little bubbles of energy bursting out towards you, little packets of expressiveness designed to engage you and carry the impact of what she was saying. She needed and wanted to share the most important things that happened to her since you last met. She was eager to hear your reactions and advice. As good friends do, she was picking up your conversation where you left off two years ago in Paris."*

Penny: *"Yes, but how did you feel?"*

Evelyn: *"I sensed her need to disregard me, to dismiss me. She did not want to take the time to explain herself to me. She had too much to share with you.*

"A different seating arrangement could have help. If we two had been sitting together, side-by-side, we could have received Kathy's communication as one. I would have experienced her Integrated Movements, mirrored them and felt in touch. Perhaps I might have melted into your relationship with her. Although I was sitting in the corner of an equilateral triangle, I was not yet an equal in the relationship. Kathy and I could not be as engaged together as you two were. We could not overcome this structure, which seemed to make you uncomfortable as well."

Penny: *"I was concerned about excluding you. I wanted us to all like each other and instead, I felt you were not engaged."*

Evelyn: *"Kathy seemed to me as if she were at the end of a long tunnel, which was hidden by her gestures. When she pulled herself together with an Integrated Movement, I could really 'see' her. I didn't consciously realize she became Integrated, I just felt that she had became 'real.' I gave in to the magnetism of her involvement in what she was describing and then we had an equal balance of three.*

"Your relationship with her seemed to wake up at that point too. I noticed you didn't need so much matching of posture once the communication moved into depth."

Penny: *"I also noticed our postures agreed at the beginning. We were trying to instantly recreate our previous closeness by setting the stage with postures."*

Evelyn: *"I compared how you both seemed to me in this phase. Kathy, who dominated the conversation, appeared much bigger, taller, thinner. You were lower down and small. Then when the involvement reached the same intensity, you both seemed to be a similar size and weight. In fact, we began to create a shape between all three of us. The balance maintained itself for the rest of the evening. We became so compatible that we easily extended our boundaries to include my husband."*

Here a new relationship was integrated into a long-term friendship. Earlier in the conversation, it looked quite different. The long-time friends become so involved that the third walked away.

Evelyn: *"I remained disengaged. My posture was a bit like a wall, upright and wide. When I let myself go, my body narrowed, focused on Kathy, my torso hollowed as if to make a receptive, concave curve, welcoming her attention. When I still did not feel involved, I made the choice to leave."*

Evelyn's reaction was instinctive. There was no room for her in this conversation. The long-term friends could have made the situation more comfortable, either by stating their need to talk together or by postponing their private talk.

LONG-TERM FRIENDSHIP: MINOR PROBLEMS

Expectations grow as a friendship deepens. Therefore, friends can have a hard time turning off a flow of communication tactfully. It is delicate business to be unavailable for sympathy and support and not cause hurt feelings.

An important skill in friendship is to realize when to disengage, either because you disagree or you can't solve a problem for your friend. This can take quite a lot of personal control. Here's an example: your friend wants your support for an idea you think is wrong. A situation like this can pose a threat to any friendship. You can still be helpful if you are willing to:

1.   Release the need to advise or agree;
2.   Become a support for your friend's self-discovery;
3.   State your views of her problem, uncritically; and
4.   Trust that her Integrated Movement discovery will reveal the best course of action.

Friends often allow for disagreements and differences without sacrificing the friendship.

❖   When an issue leads to a classic behavior pattern, treat it differently.

❖   Recognize the posture which describes your interpretation. Empathize with it.

❖   Understand what it feels like. Don't go into details, just identify the behavior and give it a name.

"Oh, this is the it-won't-work-either-way posture."

"This is the I'm-no-good, I'm-a-failure posture." Or the *"I-can't-decide-what-to-do"* one. Good friends identify these behaviors for each other, and give assurance that it will pass just as it has before.

Labeling the behavior, giving it a name (funny, hopefully), will help put it in perspective. Soon your friend will be able to identify it for herself and it will be a short-cut in your communication. Ultimately, you will both spend less time and energy dealing with it.

If you notice a behavior pattern like this on yourself, you may want to change it. You can notice how you slip into the behavior, remember how you overcame it the last time and apply those successful techniques again.[3] Gradually the behavior and the solution will become familiar to you. You become your own internalized friend who helps you whenever you want help.

We turn to different friends for counsel and support because of their expertise and life experience. One may be an artist who understands the creative process; one a businessman who can explain financial problems; another can offer technical advice. These friends form our network.

Getting good help from a friend is only one side of the coin. The other is accepting it. People have many ways to resist help and disguise their needs. For example:

"Circumstances have to be perfect before I will speak. Then I will feel entitled to ask for the close attention I know I'm going to need."

"I want people to draw me out. I direct attention away from myself and hope someone will notice. I feel resentful if they don't. Even if the exchange becomes unequal, I never say 'It's my turn.'"

"My complaints are so constant that friends avoid me."

If these inequalities persist untended, they will erode a friendship over time. To avoid this, discuss a problem you have and enlist your friend's help in solving it.

When tempers flare, friendship is tested. Even the best of friends get angry at each other. One may lose control, call names, or get nasty. No one likes this behavior, but it does demonstrate trust, a willingness to show that side of yourself. If this happens, overcome your first reaction of shock, pull yourself together and address the display with genuine honesty. Trust the person you know underneath the anger. Go back to this event later and discuss it, so that no one continues to harbor ill feelings.

The person who is the target of the anger can ease the situation with an Integrated Movement. The expression of Integrated Movement by one person helps the other person out of his/her posture.

The task is harder when two people are equally emotional. If both express their need at the same time, neither will see or hear the other. This is most common. Each person's emotional needs have to be tackled individually or they trip over each other looking for expression. To resolve this problem:

❖   Position yourselves in parallel directions;
❖   Realize that the other person's investment is as great as yours;
❖   Acknowledge the Integrated Movement of the other verbally and/or non-verbally; or
❖   See more than your own point of view.

If each of you do this, an accommodation or positive solution becomes accessible.

When the issue is "hurt feelings" rather than "out-of-control anger," the less involved person should become the listener. She does not need to mirror you but to provide steady listening support, (no shifts of posture or irrelevant gestures). The goal is to understand the hurt feelings fully because once someone feels understood, the need to express feelings changes to a need for resolution.

However, if someone persists, even after being fully heard, then she is stuck in the posture of anger and needs a physical release: a walk, deep breathing, shaking out the body, punching the air. When the emotional balance returns, your creativity will have returned. You can agree on your differences, reach a tentative solution, negotiate.

In general, you do not have to be afraid to apologize for body-level errors, like brushing off a topic, implying it is not important. An inadvertent gesture like this results in creating distance, estrangement, misunderstanding. Take your movement communication seriously to avoid hurt feelings. *"I'm sorry, I got distracted for a moment. Please go on. You were talking about your new idea for a book."*

Question: *If a friend engages you in a heated debate at an inconvenient time, how can you tactfully retreat?*

Answer: If you are being pulled into a debate and your immediate reaction is to disengage (your head and eyes look away, your body pulls back, or turns aside), shelve the debate for another time. Let your friend complete a statement, then use an Integrated Movement as you say something like *"I really have to get back to work. This argument will keep."* A series of gestures collecting oneself and preparing to go paves the way, and makes the exit less abrupt. A light-hearted comment helps too: *"Let's save the battle for the ride home."* The friend may also seem relieved and the dispute may not even come up again. It may already have served its purpose.

Question: *If I can't avoid an argument, what should I do?*

Answer: Avoid opposing postures. It is much simpler if you acknowledge the posture, release it, talk about it (gestures), then select your own suitable gestures to go beyond the argument.

Question: *Suppose my friend seems to put the relationship on the line in response to something I said?*

Answer: This posture probably comes from a feeling of unhappiness and rejection elsewhere in your friend's life. Help your friend get to the real issue.

- ❖   Defend yourself briefly;
- ❖   Reassure him of your love and friendship;
- ❖   Ask him to describe his real discomfort.

THE STRUCTURE OF FRIENDSHIP

When you are seeking a friend's help, you can ask for the kind of response you want. The following are several choices:

- ❖   A captive audience?
- ❖   An almost clairvoyant response?
- ❖   Advice?
- ❖   Understanding?
- ❖   Interpretation or criticism?
- ❖   Objectivity?
- ❖   Encouragement?

It can get complicated and even frustrating when you get advice when you want encouragement; when you get encouragement when you are looking for interpretation; when you get interpretation when you want objectivity; when you get objectivity when you want advice.

Friends also offer unsolicited help and may find it useful to identify their intention. *"One friend is so eager to help, she tells me what I need to know before I finish the story. I needed to ask her to let me tell the whole story so that I could feel it and experience the Integrated parts, the gestures and postures. Then I could understand her comments, or even find my own solutions. I was asking her to listen thoroughly before commenting. She learned to wait and let me go through the process."*

GIVING MOVEMENT FEEDBACK

"The Role Of The Observer"

Everyone can give movement feedback: beginners and experts in movement, co-counselors and psychotherapists, you and your friends. Movement is a cycle of thought, expression, reflection, new thought, new expression. Movement shows the shape and energy of the event, where and how it happens. We can say, *"Her movement toward me was sustained and elongated. It moved part of her, or all of her. She flowed with it."* We can say, *"He listened and did not move a muscle." "She looked all around when I spoke."* Register the type of movement and work with it. Describe the movement which resulted in your interpretation. The description gives your interpretation concrete support.

Giving specific feedback about movement adds shades of meaning to the words and gives them a context. It is a kind of objective truth. If the feedback rings true, your friend has a lot of new relevant information to consider in making a decision or in making changes. When the movement conveys the message perfectly, then the truth of the statement is dramatic.

The following are examples of how to give movement feedback:

- ❖ If you see only gestures, you might ask your friend: *"Can you say more about that?" "Can you go deeper into that idea?"*
- ❖ If you see posture ask: *"Is that your position?" "That's your standard posture. Are you aware of that?"*
- ❖ If you see Integrated Movement, say: *"That's important to you." "I believe that; I see how much you mean it."*

When giving movement feedback, you are listening to understand what the speaker is saying, not to think about your reaction to it. You are encouraging a creative, meaningful exchange.

REALIZING DREAMS

We each have an inner voice that needs to be heard. We each have wishes and desires, big dreams and little "mini" dreams.

When someone helps us realize a life-long goal, that person becomes a valued friend. Much of our close communication has to do with helping each other find the best way to realize our dreams. Suppose you want to help a friend fulfill his or her own dream; you just have to listen in a certain way. You have to see the dance.

Our dreams are so precious and so valued, that if we disclose them, it is often in disguised ways. We slip them into the spaces between things, spandrels of communication. We mention then while referring to some one else's success. *"If only I were like so-and-so."* Friends can help by asking questions which focus on a positive direction.

"How do you see yourself now? What would success mean?"

Your friend watches you and listens carefully as you answer. She watches the energy come back into the communication and helps you define the new steps, new actions which will lead you to success. Redirecting a person from a negative definition to a positive one is a delicate maneuver. You have to listen long enough to the negative statement to fully embrace its importance to the person, then match and acknowledge the intensity of the feelings.

You may need to initiate the shift from negative to positive. *"If you don't want this, than I guess you do want this."* We can define ourselves by what we don't want and use it as a springboard to discover what we do want. Paraphrasing the Cowardly Lion in *The Wizard of Oz*, we can say:

"I DO want opportunities to define my own scope."

"I DO want to change the way people look at business."

"I DO want to find energy alternatives."

Emphasis on the positive too soon may create resistance; "That's impossible. I couldn't do that." In friendship, people come to each other for just this shift, even if they don't realize it. With practice and success, we make the shift faster and more easily to an expanded horizon.

Recap:

❖ Initially, you saw your friend's Integrated Movement over negative verbal statements. You looked and listened carefully for indications of the dream in tiny gestures or asides in the conversation.

❖ Then, you mirrored those hints, bringing them carefully to attention; you maintained your position and posture with your statement.

❖ You acknowledged your friend's statement and accompanying Integrated Movement.

❖ You summarized and gave feedback (on the negative feelings, if necessary), with appropriate verbal and physical intensity.

❖ And you asked your friend to put negative comments in the past tense.

As the creative flow starts, your friend will feel safe to describe his dreams and connect them to real possibilities for action. Integrated Movement opens up this creative source. Your friend's energy will be totally involved in this trance-like state. Just taking it in, being a witness, is helpful; but if you can, write down the images, feelings, ideas, and practical solutions to make them even more accessible for his later use. You may want to follow up and begin a partnership or collaboration on life goals.[4]

We face an interesting paradox that at the moment we are most fully involved, we are also most easily out of self-awareness. That is where friendship comes in, helping us reach beyond ourselves.

Life-sized bronze sculpture titled, "Chance Meeting"

Life-sized bronze sculpture titled, "News"

SIX

RELATIONSHIPS

In intimate relationships, hopes, wishes and goals are shared through many years, often through a lifetime. Patterns blend and merge, postures develop and evolve. In a long-term relationship, we can "find ourselves" and achieve more than we could alone. We can 'lose ourselves' and need a period of separation from our partner to assert our individuality and experiment with new parts of our being.

How does body movement fit in? Body movement reflects everything that is happening. It is the shape and pattern of our inner voice. Integrated Movement flows in and out of tentative new ideas, patterns, gestures and postures. It keeps us in touch with what is vital and new and growing in each of us. The vulnerability and exposure Integrated Movement demonstrates encourages closeness and love.

To keep a relationship alive and vital, you need to:

❖ Recognize the postures you bring to a relationship; test their effectiveness; then change or adapt them to fit the needs of the relationship;

❖ Discover the moments of deep mutual recognition and fulfillment (shared dreams, shared activities, love-making); and

❖ Anticipate potential areas of trouble and create new patterns to avoid them.

The goal is to keep a relationship alive and vital, rather than to let it solidify into comfortable or uncomfortable roles or postures.

PRACTICING COMPATIBILITY

A telling rhythm, a flow, invariably happens when two people are in love and all is going well. It shows in their movement. Once I watched a couple on an airplane, fascinated by the 'dance' of their heads as they were talking. The timing of their turns, nods and bobs told me they were in love. When the plane had landed, we decided to share a taxi to the same hotel and our friendship began. Six months later the couple married and now, a few years later, have a home, a child, and two satisfying careers. The compatibility of their movement and their successful marriage are not a coincidence.

Of course, we can assume there have been occasional problems between them. But if my friends were aware of how their love was physically expressed in movement, they could choose to return to that state of being intentionally if problems came up. Why not practice compatibility in the same way one practices tennis, for instance? We practice the strokes and moves of sports, we can practice the strokes and moves of a loving communication. It feels wonderful to recreate that state of being when we decide to, especially when the everyday demands of life tend to exhaust our time and energy. Perhaps the successful relationships of previous generations knew this unconsciously. Let's do it on purpose.

Smooth, easy gestures create a flow, a rhythmic exchange, a balance, a readiness to get involved, a willingness to be vulnerable. These factors characterize a nourishing relationship. A loving quality enlivens the space between and around individuals. Currents of movement, pauses, a matching of body tension, complementary postures: these are all signs of emotional involvement. The degree of involvement, response, interest, or support that happens in a loving relationship can be developed.

CONFLICT

Difficulties in relationships are inevitable but they are also essential. When two people decide to share their lives they face a group of necessities: supporting a family, developing and fulfilling one's skills and talents, to name a few. The necessities are so intense that the relationship usually falls into the background, untended. Roles and tasks lead to divergent paths and the relationship can deteriorate to a separation and eventual divorce. Sometimes, growth through separation is an effective option. Another is parallel growth, for rediscovery of self and other. As we mirror and respond to each other, we promote a feeling of inevitability in relationships. The movement seems unchangeable. After a while, we kinesthetically sense and respond to signals without conscious awareness.

When there is conflict in a relationship, Integrated Movement gets pushed away or hidden beyond recognition. Gesture and posture oppose each other. We use drastic, hurtful statements. Threats fly. Ultimatums are made. We draw extreme lines to make the message very clear-cut: *"If you ever do this again, I'll never speak to you." "Marry me or good-bye." "You don't care about me, so I'm leaving."* In this way we propel ourselves and the other person into drastic action. Our postures reflect this volatile thinking, creating an impenetrable wall and making us inaccessible to ourselves and to others.

In these postures, we become rigidly defensive. Self-protection becomes our uppermost concern. We think in terms of redefining territory, property, money. What's 'yours' and 'mine' takes on a different meaning. We feel that beliefs must be protected, personal points of view defended, almost as if they were property. The degree of threat and intensity of reaction is in direct proportion to the degree of commitment of two people's lives.

In a casual relationship or one where there is no overlap of territory (although there is usually some, at least in terms of human energy), conflict is normally less intense. The boundaries or walls don't have to bounce up quite as high. Without overlapping boundaries, the fights might not even happen. Each person maintains separate values or points of view without affecting the other. They still have strong conviction, but can walk away from the fight with their lives relatively intact.

However, one goal of a long-term relationship is to encompass difference and create respect for divergent views. This is a chance to evolve a larger perspective than you might have alone. Think of it as enlarging your kinesphere (the bubble of space that surrounds your body).

Particularly when positions are stated and arguments presented, some part of you needs to step back to try and appreciate the larger perspective. Withdraw and assess. Emotions may interfere and you may need time alone to think. The distress you feel will seem to come from the outside, in fact from the other person. What seems to be outside is actually a projection from inside. Accept your need as a source of strength and think about how you are going to best cultivate it.

If, for instance, you think there is an unfair division of labor in your marriage, and state that thought, first figure out what you think would be a fair division. What do you need to do to solve the problem for yourself? Getting your partner to do more is one way, but not the only option. Similarly if you feel your partner is too demanding of your time, what time and space would you need so that you would not feel overburdened?

In this way you can begin to problem-solve. The change in thinking is tangible. Your body stops feeling tight, at odds with your head; hands, pelvis, legs begin relaxing. The new thinking seeps down from the brain, joining the heart, stomach, lungs. Breath comes in to support you. With relaxation and a consistent pattern of movement and words, you move in the direction of resolution.

Two people often need time to reflect on their own behavior in order to come back together with new appreciation for the situation. If no change results, at least you are working on the process.

Recap:

❖ Acknowledge the disagreement.

❖ Concentrate on your feelings. Find their source. You may choose to do this on your own or by talking.

❖ Step back and categorize the issue, be abstract and general.

❖ Think about what you can do for yourself, rather than being dependent on your partner to either take the blame or provide the solution.

If you can, and think it will help:

❖ Work on what you think are the other person's feelings. Put yourself in his or her shoes. Empathize. Associate. How does this make you feel? Does it frighten, anger, annoy you? Why?

You are acknowledging postures and getting to underlying reasons for them. In the search for a new thought or awareness, don't be surprised if an Integrated Movement occurs. A moment of meditation may follow. There may be tears before or during this process. Trust that these places must be explored.

RECOGNIZING YOUR POSITION IN A FIGHT

1. Again, acknowledge the fight.
2. Identify both of your postures. Articulate them.
3. Understand how the posture bears on the conflict.

It's not easy to do this work alone. A therapist or talented friend can help a lot by pointing out your posture, mirroring it, questioning it. This way you get a chance to separate from your posture, to actually look at it, talk about it and gain insights.

To illustrate a clash of gesture and posture:

"It was only when we went to see Jasper, a therapist, that I become aware of my nonchalant posture. I was telegraphing an 'I-don't-care message.' I was only aware of how hard I was trying, gestures."

The goal in breaking up postures is to create a pattern of interference like a moiré pattern.[1] The new perception depends on being able to see the pattern. Music demonstrates this very well. The juxtaposition of two rhythmic patterns creates a hemiola. It is a transition when accidentally all of the established patterns collide. Out of the chaos and seeming conflict, a new pattern emerges. In the same way, an Integrated Movement occurs when all the dispersed energy collides. It is the pattern in a relationship, when the divergent paths meet, and harmony is released between them. Look for these patterns, look for these "accidents" and take advantage of them.

To Gain Perspective:

1. Pause and look at the whole picture. Move away from where you were standing. Judge your posture as someone else would.
2. Describe how you see yourself. Do the same for the other if you can.
3. See if there is an overall pattern into which you both fit. Stop there. You have done enough to focus your perspective.

If you wish, go on and:

4. Describe each other's positions (physically and/or verbally).
5. Can you agree you have a problem to solve, and identify what it is?
6. Can you find a temporary, small, modest solution to try?
7. Can you agree to do something which will make you both feel better, and return to the discussion later from different postures?

The principles are:

❖ When conflict occurs, create distance to see yourself, to experience yourself. (A walk in the woods, a visit with a friend.)

❖ Work on a solution for yourself to help you feel positive about the relationship.

❖ Have a friend identify when your Integrated Movements occur as you discuss the problem. Use this information to know where your needs are.

The goal of a relationship is good sharing, good communication, respect and love. Along the way we are confronted with ourselves, our needs, our deficiencies and dreams, over and over again. Beware of the danger of letting one issue carry the importance of the whole relationship.

To help you gain more control, ask yourself:

❖ Can I talk about this in a non-threatening way?

❖ Can I separate from my own needs/dependency long enough to listen to my partner and watch his/her Integrated Movement?

❖ Do I need to air my feelings with a good friend first?

In a workshop, one woman felt so far from marital harmony, she could barely remember it. Her associate asked her to remember a time when she and her husband were very happy together. As she did this, the feelings came flooding back. Then when she spoke about her needs and her desire to change things, she had released her "offended" posture and could speak with Integrated Movements.

If we can only establish some agreement, perhaps we could again experience that rhythmic harmony, the easy quality of being in step as we walk along, talking about anything, feeling the underlying compatibility, that quality of ease that is the essence of the relationship.

UNDERSTANDING INTEGRATED MOVEMENT HELPS RELATIONSHIPS

'Active listening' is the process of paraphrasing what someone has said in order to ensure accurate understanding. In the same way, a slight mirroring of Integrated Movement simultaneously or just after the speaker, expresses empathy and acknowledges the other's feelings. It shows you heard, understood and recognized the importance of the communication. It replaces pitying or sympathetic gestures which can be inappropriate to the depth of the situation and the emotions of the speaker. Mirroring Integrated Movement also keeps you attentive and undistracted by your own inner thoughts.

In a close relationship it is hard to stay neutral, particularly when listening to something which may be personally upsetting. Your natural impulse is to either react or 'tune out.' Things you can do to be more supportive are:

❖ Put yourself in the other person's shoes quickly and as best you can so that you can understand from her point of view;

❖ Maintain a good balanced posture. (Do not shrink or withdraw.) Stay with the person so that he/she feels contacted;

❖ Mirror, reinforce. Make physical contact if it seems to help. Show you are not going to react with your own personal needs immediately.

❖ If the intensity of the conflict increases, match movement, as described above. Then state that you can listen better in a lower intensity. Physical contact will reassure and help the person calm down.

❖ Your response to Integrated Movement will show continued support. We all need outlets for emotions and frustrations. We need our close partners to listen even when we are not well-composed.

WHEN INTEGRATED MOVEMENTS ARE NOT ACKNOWLEDGED

By refusing to see Integrated Movement, we are actively resisting change. We feel that we have our roles to maintain. Roles and postures are like an old suit of clothes, easy to step into, comfortable. In a close relationship, we even insist on them. *"We agreed to this role, how dare you try to change!"* We won't let the "strong" partner be vulnerable, even for a moment. We maintain our own position at all cost, guarding it with constant vigilance. We use blinders to guard against seeing Integrated Movement.

In a fight, we think: *"The words are familiar. I know this argument. I desperately don't want to go over this territory again."* In this scenario, we do everything possible to avoid seeing Integrated Movement: squirm, cough, interrupt, look away. The Integrated Movement, the emotional expression, is lost and the person rightly feels unheard. No one is to blame. This is a natural reaction. Frustration is the inevitable result.

As the communicator, we give signs: a breath, a sigh, an emotional signal. They are important cues. In those moments we sense rejection or acceptance which depends on the other's attention to Integrated Movement.

Just when we want the process to be automatic, it is not. No one taught us when it is necessary to mirror our partner, or how best to support this creative process.[2]

It helps to use a gesture to alert your partner to the importance of your communication. Use a nice safe gesture and ask for exactly what you need: time, encouragement, sympathy, involvement.

When we think we cannot expose our own vulnerability, we reduce our Integrated Movement around our partner for fear of disrupting the established roles. We also avoid seeing our partner's Integrated Movement as a way of rejecting intimacy. We insist on the familiar role, even if it is not satisfying. In order to express our needs and vulnerability safely, we might turn outside the relationship where it is easier to give up the assumed role.

An 'outside' relationship can be a kind of gesture in the context of the primary one. It creates a way to reapproach the primary relationship with renewed love, bringing alive what had become habit, what was being taken for granted. An affair can give an affirmation of self which leads to growth. It also signals that something needs work in the relationship, in oneself.[3]

❖ Check the parameters you have established in the new relationship. What are they telling you about yourself?

❖ What were your old expectations? Can they be negotiated?

❖ Does this mean separating to grow, or expanding the boundaries of the existing relationship? Can you incorporate the new discoveries into the old context or must you create a new one?

We can never hand over the responsibility for our growth to someone else, but we can get help from myriad resources: friends, work, painting classes, massage therapists, support groups.

Question: *What do you do when a husband and wife have roles they have practiced for thirty years? How does one find the Integrated Movements, the fresh thoughts?*

Answer: The awareness of a need for change is a powerful motivator.

As long as you realize that the desired change starts with yourself, you have every reason to expect success. Old patterns are perhaps the ones in most need of change. The more individual growth that takes place within a relationship, the more chance two people have to appreciate and enjoy each other. The willingness to take responsibility for your own success or failure is very healthy in a long-term relationship. You will find that new roles emerge as you work on yourself.

Question: *How do I know the difference between a supportive listening posture and a defensive / protective one that doesn't let me respond?*

Answer: Ask yourself if you can move out of your posture easily. Do you feel receptive or judgmental in this posture?

❖ Try a slouched posture with your arms and legs locked. Keep a focused gaze. Is this a good, detached way for you to observe Integrated Movement? Does it help you pay attention when your body is more removed from the speaker?

❖ Now try a loose, more narrowly focused posture. Do ripples of response flow through you so that mirroring is effortless and you are more sensitive to the Integrated Movement?

Questioning and testing for your own receptivity is the most important evaluation. One posture is a leaned-back, considered, analytic attitude, closed off to keep oneself paying attention and not interrupting. A subtle change could make this same posture seem frustrated, annoyed, unreceptive. Check in with your feelings honestly and you will know.

Don't be afraid to ask the speaker: "Do you feel I am listening carefully? Is this okay?" Negotiating at this level can be very helpful, showing your willingness to hear and understand.

A frustrated posture is likely to be made up of many body angles, and accompanying annoyed gestures, like sudden tense movements.

Question: *How do I know if I am in a receptive posture?*

Answer: A receptive posture allows you to more easily share your partners feelings. Do you feel empathy for his or her position? Even if you disagree, can you imagine feeling this way yourself? Put aside your personal reactions and search for accurate understanding.

Question: *When I speak, I think I tend to use offensive gestures. Why?*

Answer: You might be using pointing, piercing, or poking gestures for emphasis, or to enumerate specific grievances but you are making it difficult for the listener. Over use of gestures get in the way of being heard. They can become accusing and irritating in personal discussion. When you find yourself putting too much intensity into gestures rather than seeking the Integrated Movement, stop. Take time to find what is behind the intensity. It's usually frustration or annoyance. Once you have found the cause, make a statement which outlines the whole situation. Then the emphasis on specifics may be appropriate.

One way to check if a gesture is offensive is to amplify it and describe its action. Its message will come across loud and clear. You can check postures too by exaggeration. Your postures can be subtle yet disruptive. If you sense you are having an undesired effect on someone, change your posture and/or your gesture, regardless of the message. The reason that the posture or gesture is offensive is irrelevant. The change itself may eliminate the problem.

Question: *Why do we limit ourselves by postures and gestures?*

Answer: Because they are obvious and easy tools of communication. They feel safe and familiar. Until now, we have not been familiar with Integrated Movement as a viable option.

Question: *What do I do to support my partner's Integrated Movement?*

Answer: Pay close attention. You will hear, see and feel the communication, and have a real understanding of the feelings being expressed. Do not get upset by what you hear. Do not rush in to respond, to explain, to fix, to defend. Whether you agree or not is not the point, whether he is right or not is not the point. The point is that your partner is now revealing himself to you. He is vulnerable. You must at least offer true support for that risk. Acknowledge what is said by your seriousness, your silence or your words. The empathy and support you offer will be returned in trust and closeness.

Question: *How do I make certain that my needs are met?*

Answer: Once you have given support, it may be perfectly appropriate to shift over to your reactions, to air your side and reveal your need. If so, do it. If not, simply acknowledge that the depth and feeling of the communication felt satisfying. When the time comes that you need careful attention, be sure to ask for it. "Please listen the way I did when we spoke about x." If possible, explain what you did to make that conversation work better than it had in the past.

The knowledge that each of you can now trust the other to hear what is important to you and not dismiss it is deserves a celebration. While we cannot always meet another person's needs fully, we can listen with understanding.

THE ROLE OF SUPPORTIVE FRIENDS

When a couple is experiencing difficulty, they tend to turn to friends for advice and help. A friend can help you discover what you cannot see in your love relationship or partnership. Usually we start by wanting the friend to justify our position and give us unequivocal support. When we have exhausted that direction, we can then have a friend point out our postures, gestures and Integrated Movements. Now our friend is really helping us find a solution, going beyond loyalty. We are often too angry and there is too much at stake to be detached enough to observe ourselves.

Example: *"A close friend was in a badly troubled relationship. I asked him to describe his long-term vision for himself and his companion. He seemed to do this. (Great, I thought. He has taken me seriously.) He then went into a litany of everything his partner did wrong and how she wouldn't allow for a positive future. As I watched and listened, I saw no Integrated Movements, only postures.*

"When he started to describe his own needs, I saw Integrated Movements, but I became unsympathetic. I began to examine my own thoughts. I explored my posture and found that I could empathize more with my friend's partner than with him. Thinking about her, I felt she wanted his understanding, not his criticism. My friend's anger only served to create a gulf between them, and also made it hard for him to accept my efforts to help. As I explained this to him, his posture changed; he relaxed and became much more receptive. This showed me that he was open to advice and I felt useful and appreciated."

BREATHING SPACE

"Robert and I were on different sides of an issue. We tried to talk about it. He chose a chair far away from me. We talked unsuccessfully. I invited him closer. We tried again, but the psychological distance remained. The issue was emotionally loaded and each of us too entrenched to solve it ourselves. We decided we needed an intermediary: someone who could say, "It's your turn. Now it's your turn." We saved the issue for a therapy session.

"The distance we felt now became evident in my discomfort while listening. No one could have spoken to my closed-off, twisted away posture and ticking, annoyed gestures. If I had been the only person in the room, Robert would have stopped talking. The therapist controlled what was happening by being receptive to Robert's communication. After a while I realized that I was no longer a bundle of averted gestures and hostile postures, but was riveted, focused, listening intensively and seeking meaning in every word. Obviously this was an important communication. We were negotiating deep values. It mattered. It was not a casual conversation."

In this example, Robert and his wife, Cynthia, were actually sitting side by side, facing the therapist. This seating arrangement promoted a unified focus and the emotional content was deflected to the therapist. The therapist pointed out that Cynthia and Robert's postures were opposite. One was over-protective; one overly demanding. The extremes balanced each other beautifully, but were not functional. The couple acknowledged their extreme postures and agreed to work toward greater balance.

Sometimes relationships need real distance so that each person can re-establish personal boundaries, find one's familiar, singular self and see the other free from projections. We need to hear our childhood voices again, without the clutter of roles, postures and assumptions that have developed during the course of the relationship. We seek affirmation by seeing ourselves in new mirrors outside the relationship, where less is at stake.

"My wife and I valued our independence. After a time our relationship became very cold and distant. We grew so far apart that all that was left were the postures of self-sufficiency. Soon, I became involved with someone else. In that new relationship, I found the emotional involvement I was looking for, but missed the independence I had enjoyed before. From this experience, I gained an understanding of how to develop the emotional side of my marriage and decided to do so."

When each marriage partner is actively working on his/herself, a new security and understanding can develop in the relationship. Each has a more rounded view, more independence, more personal power. As each person gets stronger, joint decision-making improves. They each find support in the relationship, rather than feeling the need to destroy it in order to somehow "prove" themselves.

Question: *"Why is it easier to be vulnerable in a non-committed relationship?"*

Answer: In a marriage or other committed relationship, you are building a structure. Your individual roles are integral to the whole relationship. You cannot lay them aside. In a secondary relationship, however, none of this is at stake. Feelings are accepted with few consequences. If you can understand what needs are being filled outside the relationship, you can work towards creating them within it.

❖ Be introspective. Find your own feelings. Identify your needs. (The chances are that your partner has unfulfilled needs too.)

❖ If you find yourself wanting to find fault with your partner, pinpoint the reasons; i.e., *"I blame him for not being supportive enough."* Realizing that you need more personal support, you can now begin to problem-solve. In this example, perhaps you could develop a support network.

❖ Help your partner identify what his needs are. Don't blame yourself for not fulfilling them. Instead, try to find comfortable ways to help.

PROJECTIONS

Projections are a subtle danger to a relationship. They are images and opinions we hold about ourselves and those we project to others. Projections are our "shadow" postures; ones we have not fully accepted as part of ourselves.[4] The mind sets up an image based on who I think I am and who I think you are, then tries to make all information fit into these roles. In a successful relationship, projections evolve naturally and become assimilated.[5]

Example: *"I projected weakness to him. As far as I was concerned, I was the strong one, and he weak, yet I yearned for him to be strong. I thought if I changed my role as the strong one, our relationship might improve.*

"Then one night when I suggested we get together, he said he had a date and would not break it. I was furious until I remembered that I had wanted him to be strong. The problem, I realized, was that now I was faced with his assertiveness and I didn't like it. I felt my posture settle into outrage, but controlled myself. A deep breath took me past my first reaction. I relaxed. I told him that I felt we had potential for a good relationship. He said he was glad that I didn't overreact or think that our relationship was over.

"We now needed to test the strength of our bond. Since my feelings had made such a sudden shift, I became aware of how much I had been projecting. The projection, 'I am strong, you are weak,' did not let me see him as a person until our bond was nearly broken.

"As our relationship progressed, he began to take charge and I became the helpless one. He decided to stop seeing the other person but never told me. He felt he still had to play games, because it had worked well before.

"I don't blame him for not trusting me at that point. We were looking at a serious commitment. We were talking about marriage. Before, I was afraid of commitment. Now he was. We were finally seeing a whole other side of each other.

"By experiencing the potential loss of the relationship, I became ready to make a bigger commitment. He had his own issues to overcome. I thought, 'perhaps if he continues to see honesty and openness in me, he can do the same.'

"When this change began, body awareness helped me control the moment of panic. The panic was a visceral response. I had to go to the body to counteract it."

The example of strong versus weak roles is a familiar one. In a movement workshop we played them out, one pair at a time. We pushed and pulled at each other as we spoke in totally direct language: *"How strong I am." "How weak you are."* We changed roles. We used the actual content of our lives as the context of the exercise.[6] We examined how neither extreme presents the whole story of a personality. A part of ourselves encompasses the projected persona (posture), but there is a counterpart. (My weak, helpless self has a strong, domineering counterpart.)

To experience this yourself:
1. Talk about a strong/weak situation until your role stands out.
2. Play yourself for a while.
3. Then play the counterpart.
4. Listen to the dialogue and feel the physical participation.

Once you have learned about the other side of yourself, you will not project that side of your being with such intensity.

Why Projections Are Dangerous:

- ❖ They replace a true sense of self.
- ❖ One reacts to the projections not to the person.
- ❖ One resents the person being herself.
- ❖ Love can vanish with the projection.

Projections, like postures, create signposts for discovering the direction of growth. Assimilate the projections, understand their origin (probably in childhood), find your capacities and create a more useful way of thinking about yourself.

Roles can best be seen when amplified into stories. Weave your projection of yourself and your partner into an allegorical story. If you find this story at odds with the person you are becoming, invent a new one. (It doesn't need to be realistic. You just need to create the fantasy with your partner.) If no story emerges, you may be at the end of a journey and starting a new one.

The process of dissolution of a relationship has great learning potential. There is usually a dramatic shift in projections. The roles switch. The sense of power changes. What was in the shadow comes to light.

Case History: Tom felt depressed. *"Life has no meaning. We have all we want and yet we have nothing."* Sally withdrew. To herself, she said *"I know what I want, and I am not at all satisfied yet."* Each posture intensified. The more unhappy Tom got, the more Sally withdrew. Finally Tom said *"I'm leaving."* This was an assertive stance, a healing action for Tom. He moved from posture to Integrated Movement. He figured out what he needed to do and did it. This jolted Sally out of complacency. Tom was no longer the "victim." They were no longer threatening or accusing each other, they had moved on to action.

Sally was miserable, but Tom was now angry. Their postures did not stop all at once, however. *"I'm leaving!"*

"Good! I'm fine on my own. You make too many rules, just like my father." (Blame and projection. I see you as my father, not as yourself.)

Indifference led to threats, shouting, doors slamming, stalking out of the room. They were far from any understanding. Soon, exhausted, they began to communicate from a place of need. He said, *"I don't think I can give you what you want."* She said, *"I have new dreams. I am only beginning to understand what they are."*

Now they were working on the real issues of the relationship. They both looked and felt sad. *"I'm in pain."* And the other said, *"So am I."* Thus they began a healing process which allowed them to remain friends despite their ultimate decision to separate.

HEALING ANCIENT WOUNDS

A long-term relationship is likely to carry old, perhaps partially unhealed wounds. Assimilating and discarding them feels good and will bring new life to the relationship.

Build towards the understanding you want in small increments. Remember to use your Integrated Movement to establish your point of view; use it to discover what you need to say. Use it as a wrench to unseat limited thinking and to expand how you listen to your partner. Use it also to break the pattern of an old wound which has turned into a static posture.

In general, ancient wounds provoke more violent arguments. One partner becomes highly emotional and the other is likely to freeze and be unable to respond with an Integrated Movement. Your need to be heard escalates, especially in arguments which traditionally have caused outbursts. To avoid this, admit your feelings before they become entrenched. See if your feelings seem accurate to the situation. When you are both calm and have a better understanding of the old issues, relegate them to the past.

Two hurt people coming together is a delicate process. The very pain and discomfort each mirrors pushes them apart like opposing magnets, as each one looks past the other for the solution. Talking and listening, when it happens in the right atmosphere and with sensitivity, is the most common solution.

Words are symbols and carry a lot of meaning. The distance melts. To reach this state, first recognize the painful state. Then recreate a feeling of wholeness from somewhere in your experience. Mastering this gives you faith in finding a solution. The first sign of wholeness is Integrated Movement. Watch for it in the other person, empathize, no matter what is said.

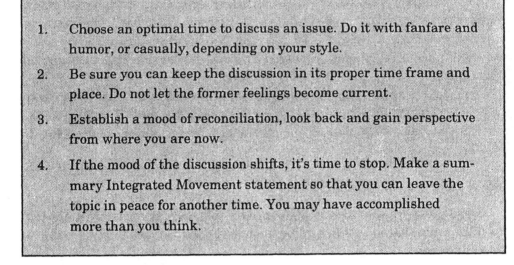

1. Choose an optimal time to discuss an issue. Do it with fanfare and humor, or casually, depending on your style.

2. Be sure you can keep the discussion in its proper time frame and place. Do not let the former feelings become current.

3. Establish a mood of reconciliation, look back and gain perspective from where you are now.

4. If the mood of the discussion shifts, it's time to stop. Make a summary Integrated Movement statement so that you can leave the topic in peace for another time. You may have accomplished more than you think.

EXPLORING POSTURES IN MARRIAGE

Roles we bring to marriage are ones we have been developing all our lives. We bring our parents' roles, our reactions to those roles and our childhood fantasies. We are not free of these until we have discovered them in ourselves, faced them and developed new behaviors. This is the adolescence of the relationship. Everyone has a vision of a Prince or Princess Charming. It can be fascinating to ask your partner to describe the qualities he/she was looking for in an "ideal mate." This is something a married couple seldom talks about, but I did.

"Someone who loves the outdoors and art and is deep," said my husband. We laughed.

"I was looking for a scientist, an intellectual and a good skier. I wanted a 'different' lifestyle." The possible fulfillment of these vague and hidden ideals propelled us along in our courtship, despite many differences. We had never articulated or even consciously admitted these expectations.

In general, once married, a whole new set of expectations become operative. Complementary postures enable each partner in the marriage to feel supported and to act. Having your posture acknowledged lets you work in a receptive environment, with humor, toward a full understand of one another. Two people help each other become what they each want to be and attain the roles the other once imagined. As you build a new life, you each pay attention to the role you play for the other, but perhaps don't notice what is being sacrificed.

OVERVIEW OF A SUCCESSFUL RELATIONSHIP

These steps can help smooth out unnecessary rough spots in a relationship.
1. Make an inventory of your postures in a relationship. Do they still work for you or do they need updating?
2. Nourish your changing self. Do you have enough time alone? Do you have enough time with your partner? Is an attitude of your partner's getting in the way of your own self-development? Is your attitude about yourself getting in your way?
3. Be alert to trouble spots in your relationship and the need to establish new patterns. Beware of reacting to new needs with old postures.
4. Find ways to support the first tentative steps into a new dream; help build it. Can you wholeheartedly support your partner's growth without feeling threatened? Acknowledge that you may need to build a new dream even without your partner's support. Our own needs and emotions often blind us to the potential within our grasp.

Two people who live together become very sensitive to subtle physical and emotional changes. Take advantage of this by addressing what you observe.

❖ If you see more concentration than usual, less movement, or rigidity of the body, register these, think about them and talk about them.

❖ If you meet denial (*"Nothing is wrong,"*), show the other person what he looks like to gain a shared perception. *"But you seem tense,"* will help the partner understand what you are seeing and what he is "saying."[7]

A TOUCH OF IMAGERY

A creative way to enliven your relationship and nourish your changing self at the same time is to find an image with the quality you want to feel and let it permeate your life.

❖ First, find the image.
❖ Then, connect it to your everyday life.
❖ Next, meditate on the feeling of it. Consecrate the moment somehow; share it, write it down.

The Image: *"Sunlight glinting on water, in a majestic mountain range, rapidly flowing streams and waterfalls."*

The Personal Connection: "I want fun and brightness, a glistening and clear quality in my life; to feel invigorated, revitalized and renewed. I want to feel this every day."

The Image: *"Walking on the beach, moonrise and sunset at the same time, balancing in the sky; the feeling of fullness and peace, wholeness and connectedness to nature."*

The Personal Connection: *"I want to feel secure and calm. I want to be wise and promote environmental awareness."*

The Image: *"Fire always changing and bringing people together, healing."*

The Connection: *"I want to feel the healing quality in my life. I feel a moment of spiritual intensity."*

You may feel a bit awed by the size of your vision. Allow it. It harms no one. It benefits you and others.

Life-size bronze sculpture titled, "Big Sister"

SEVEN

FAMILY

Communication within families, of necessity, is set in postures. Roles allow parents to be parents and children to be children. Unfortunately, roles also tend to keep parents and children from knowing each other and adapting.

In each phase of development, roles undergo change. In a child's early years, both mother and father are protecting, guiding and modeling behavior for the child. If parents continue in the protective role as the child grows, the independence of the child is threatened. Allowing the role to become excessive can inhibit a more mature relationship from developing. As children grow into adults they have to shed their previous roles, just as lobsters shed their ectoskeletons. They need to break their habitual patterns of relating.

The transition to adulthood is perhaps the most difficult. We have arrived when we have confidence in our own decisions and actions and do not rely on or rebel against parental guidance. My friend Reva, sophisticated in movement analysis, was consciously taking this step.

Reva was considering studying psychology and presented her thoughts to her parents. She paid conscious attention to her Integrated Movement and had even introduced her parents to it. Support for her plans was very important to her. Reva's father's verbal reaction was: *"You already are highly trained. How will this additional course of study help you earn a living?"* As he spoke, Reva gestured to her mother to notice his movement. At once, they all laughed. Reva's father realized he was speaking more from a posture, his own need, not from Reva's. Then, he shifted from the expanded chest, hands-on-hip posture, to a more relaxed adjustment of the torso. His sincere concern became more evident in the new posture, when he rephrased, beginning with: *"I'm not necessarily right, but this is how it seems to me."*

Reva had never felt support or approval from her father. This time it was different. *"At last my father stopped trying to protect me by dictating his choices to me. I did not feel I had to run away from him."*

By being attuned to her father's Integrated Movement, Reva understood his personal investment and sincerity. She did not feel it necessary to combat the posture. Although she may have been disappointed not to get the instant approval or understanding she wanted, she no longer needed to feel rebellious while secretly wondering if he was right. The new recognition created a strong bond of equality between parent and child.

FAMILY MYTHS

Family myths are the stories created to develop and maintain roles. Myths often stay viable even when they become outmoded. They can create unrecognized tensions and sometimes even become self-fulfilling statements. How can we change family myths so that we can develop more satisfying family relationships?

- ❖ Separate and identify the posture; your own, the family's.
- ❖ Align with your designated family posture. Perhaps use humor to ease its power over you.
- ❖ Confront the expected behavior directly. Again, show that you are not perpetuating the myth.

For example, you are always accused of being late. You are "the recalcitrant child." If you are ever late you are proving the point. On the other hand, if you are on time, it is looked upon as the exception and does not change the established myth. After a while, everyone expects you to be late. Then, if you are, it fits nicely into a pattern. Being on time has no reward, so there is little motivation. The pattern remains. What can you do?

Response #1: *"I am not always late!"* implies defensiveness and tends to prove the opposite point. Your denial, accompanied by your childish posture, feels stuck, uncomfortable, makes you squirmy, adamant. It is ineffective for you under the circumstances.

Response #2: *"Oh, you are worried that we won't be on time. But we want to be and will be."* This takes you out of the myth and returns you to the moment. It would feel good to say this and it certainly is reassuring for others to hear it. You have met the challenge with a mature, direct posture.

Response #3: *"Oh gosh, another chance to be late. How long does it take to get to your house, twenty minutes?"* (You know it takes two hours.) *"Just kidding, okay, we'll try."* Exaggerate the posture as a way of breaking down the myth.

Response #4: A sophisticated analysis of the event: *"Are you really worried about my being late, or are you tense about the whole event?"* (Expect denial, but you have made your point anyway.) *"I will do my best to be on time. I understand the tension and feel it too. It is probably what makes me late in the first place."* Here the task is to be true to yourself. You are addressing the event sincerely. You are no longer in posture but in Integrated Movement.

I am sure you can picture how the body changes with each response.

THE MOTHER, THE DAUGHTER AND THE ROAST

In this story there are several examples of changing family roles. The hostess, who was the mother of the bride-to-be, was wrapped up in intellectual discussions with the father-in-law-to- be. She told me: *"I was so engrossed in what I was saying that I completely forgot to turn on the roast! The whole dinner was a mess because I was more concerned about the conversation. My daughter did not follow me around helping as she usually did, checking up on me. She deserted me. (A clue to the value of the experience was just articulated!)*

"We turned the roast on 'high' and it burned to a crisp. The vegetables too were inedible. My son finally said: 'when it's my turn, Mom, could we please go to a restaurant!' But why did all this happen?" she asked.

The mother-daughter relationship was changing, as the events clearly demonstrated. There was the obvious metaphor about the desertion of the daughter indicating the fear of being replaced by a mother-in-law. The event, which was all taken in good will, did have serious meaning. Roles had shifted. The symbols were clear. In reviewing the evening, the daughter reassured the mother of her love. The "ruined" dinner served as a catalyst to allow a discussion of the important shifts in role that were taking place.

The roles we take on as parents are strongly influenced by what we remember from our own childhood...the way our parents treated us and how we felt as children. We try not to repeat our own painful childhood experiences when we ourselves are parents. A friend of mine told me that her writing teacher reprimanded her son who was visiting the class. My friend felt the criticism was too harsh. Although she did not intervene, she became upset, remembering a similar circumstance in her own past.

I told her that I would be glad to give her Integrated Movement feedback on this experience although I didn't know if it would help. As she talked, she found connections to her own childhood: *"I did things as a child which I had been told*

were allowed. Then I was punished for doing them. No one ever let me explain.
I don't want this to happen to my child."

My friend said she had been a quiet, studious child who enjoyed playing by herself. Her son, on the other hand, is full of energy, dare-devilish, bouncy and boisterous. (What a difference!)

As I watched her movement, I could see that my friend became more Integrated when she spoke about her own feelings than when she talked about the experience with her son. I told her this. She realized that if she addressed her own childhood feelings, she would be better able to understand her own child's needs and not confuse the two. She now felt freer to respond honestly, moment-to-moment to her child, not to her memories of herself.

Parenting is about finding your footing in a new situation, creating a position, maintaining it, changing it when necessary and continually nourishing it by your honest conviction. Parenting becomes a balance point which can be easily dislodged. Attention to Integrated Movement can keep you from locking yourself into positions you don't believe. Integrated Movement helps a parent establish discipline from conviction, rather than from rules. Rules are only good when they work. When they are tested, they need to be substantiated with the intensity of Integrated Movement.

DISCIPLINE

Children are pretty good at figuring out the rules and then how to get around them. I watched a teenager manipulate his mother into allowing him to sleep at a friend's. "Whatever you think is best is okay with me." His lack of resistance encouraged her positive response. But there are those difficult times when you must say "no," and hold to it. If your child becomes upset, it may be hard for you to remain calm. You may be presented with a challenging stance and your patience may be tested to the limit. Suggest that you will listen to his side of the issue calmly, if he will do the same for you.

❖ Be as non-confrontational as possible.

❖ Stay focused. Explain your rationale from an Integrated physical place. Do not let annoyance and posture creep in as it will weaken your message.

❖ Make it very clear when you have finished and shift your posture, so that the topic shifts.

Example: *"'Can I go meet my friends downtown?' my daughter asked. 'My homework is nearly done and I can do my chores after six when I get back.' This request happened the day after a sleep-over party was held at our home. My* *answer was clearly 'no'. In fact, I felt angry that she asked. Everything in me wanted to explode. 'Stay composed,' I thought. 'Breathe.' I forced myself to be reasonable as I presented my reasons for saying 'no.' To my great satisfaction, I managed to stay calm and held my ground in a way that felt good to me."*

This method can work especially well if you have trouble disciplining your children. (It keeps you from losing your temper and throwing a tantrum yourself!) By staying calm, you not only keep the channels of communication open, but you fulfill an important part of being a parent. If you control a first angry reaction and present a more tempered one, you are helping the child diffuse tensions. You are also "containing" the child, thereby providing security. With time, you may even be thanked and told you were right in setting limits.

When a couple becomes parents, their relationship to each other changes. In one situation, the husband felt excluded from his wife's relationship to their son. At the same time, the wife felt the husband was not interested in the infant. Each posture perpetuated the other. Years later, when the father-son relationship blossomed, the wife withdrew from the relationship, paralleling the earlier behavior of the father.

To avoid this outcome, check out postures as soon as you notice them: *"I get the feeling you are not interested in Dan and all the little changes that happen."*

"That's because I feel excluded every time you go into raptures over a gurgle. It's like you are saying, 'leave us alone'."

A serious need is being expressed. Make adjustments. For instance:

❖ "Why not spend time with Dan when I'm not at home so that you can feel what a one-to-one is like with him?"

❖ "I'll try to be more aware and include you.

❖ "Let's make time for ourselves and have a baby-sitter more often."

Another example:

"I was expressing anger with Bob the same way my mother got angry at my father. This realization made me wonder if I was justified. Could it be that I was not trusting Bob's sensitivity with our daughter and therefore was actively excluding him from the relationship?

"This went on, even when I asked for Bob's help, knowing I was floundering and out of control in my own behavior. I could not continue to exclude him when it was convenient for me, then call upon him when I needed him, expecting him to have the confidence to act. We were both beginning to believe our postures. Luckily, we were able to stop. I practiced letting Bob be in charge. In later years, his parenting strengths were vital."

The change was so far-reaching that the couple's own relationship improved. Ideally, parenting combines the best of two people. Each parent should be alert to problematic postures, notice signs, and be willing to change.

FAMILIARITY BREEDS POSTURES AND GESTURES

The family structure promotes roles: mother, father, siblings. They provide comfort and stability. They are predictable and familiar and can be comfortable and supportive.

It is wonderful to know your favorite dessert will appear invariably at a family dinner; that a telephone call saying you are always welcome at the family "homestead," means, how about a visit soon...or the happy sound of recognition when your parents hear your voice on the telephone at three AM. We come to take these patterns for granted. But when we want to establish ourselves independently, we resist them and find them annoying. The familiarity becomes discomfort when we want to cut through the dense postures and gestures, to address topics outside the usual patterns.

DEVELOPING NEW WAYS TO RELATE

Create "excuses" to really talk to each other. Find an environment which offers new opportunities to interact, new things to do, see, talk about. It may take some careful planning, but it is worth it. Eliminate the typical distractions.

Perhaps, for a change, you could suggest that everyone go to New England for Thanksgiving, rather than deciding who will make the Turkey. Celebrate an anniversary at a resort. The cost will be less than making a party and the experience more memorable.

Bring games and puzzles. These provide an external focus and an excuse for lively, spontaneous interaction. Challenging board games, for example, promote laughter and can bring hidden talents to light. (A game of catch on the lawn will do nicely.) The important thing is the physical involvement, focusing attention away from the self and onto a task begins to shift the relationships. The full body participates. Gestures and postures slip into Integrated Movements. People get a fresh look at each other. The mind clears and we are ready to relate in new ways. Playing games also helps balance the dominant family members with the more retiring ones, making everyone temporarily equal.

A group activity provides a background of harmony. If you like to fish, do that with a family member. The free time between casting and changing lures will provide time for easy communication. If a difficult or emotional issue needs attention, an external focus diffuses the tension of confrontation. Visiting a museum and critiquing the work can raise the very issues that need to be addressed. Here, the background itself enhances the communication.

Whenever possible, design seating arrangements to facilitate communication. Make it comfortable for people, but not so comfortable that the traditional roles dominate. Put those who annoy each other far apart. Pay respect to honored guests and hosts, using the "power spots," heads and centers of tables.

Then, introduce topics of real interest: politics, art, education, to generate Integrated Movement involvement. Stir up opinions. Make sure everyone is involved. Don't skirt the big, important topics either, even though one often feels constraints around these. *"What ever happened with that meeting you told us about? How did things work out?"* For the most part, people will respond positively to your concern and interest.

If you want to establish meaningful rather than superficial communication, do not wait for others to invite you to speak. Don't feel somewhat offended that the conversation is irrelevant to you and you are not included. Discuss what is of interest to you. Test the waters with a gesture to show sensitivity and leave a path open for retreat. Allow your interest to manifest in an Integrated Movement.

Because of roles, discussions which cross generations can be awkward. Have you ever been with someone you love, yet found it hard to have a conversation? A grandparent? An aging parent? Think about it. What would interest this person? Stories of his past, career memories, special experiences? When you stir the memory, you stir the Integrated Movement and recreate positive feelings.

By focusing our interest on their accomplishments and their past, we are rewarded by an oral history of the family and its traditions. Activating Integrated Movement helps keep the self engaged in living.

If you know your uncle likes building things, lead the discussion there. Watch for the Integrated Movements. They are cues to lead you on in the conversation. By acknowledging and responding to them, you attain a feeling of closeness and a sense of satisfaction from the communication.

Too often we focus mainly on the logistics and pragmatic aspects of our relationships and leave the feelings unspoken. We lose valuable opportunities

to know the people who are most important to us. A sense of history and identity
is then lost.

> To facilitate any discomfort you may have, make a sequence of pos-
> ture, gesture and Integrated Movements to help you to move
> gracefully between levels of communication. Announce your inten-
> tions with postures. Make all the polite gestures, then introduce
> your meaningful material.

The quality and style of sharing differs throughout life, especially within
family structures and roles. However, with maturity we can take responsibility
for creating the quality of the relationship which will most easily promote the
depth of communication we want. A satisfying communication might also be
just a personal recognition of a beautiful moment together. It is impossible to
know any one person one hundred percent, even our closest loved one, but a
different lingering sadness remains when more might have been shared, more
might have been understood.

If you have real trouble engaging a loved-one in a conversation which goes
beyond the usual chatter, consider structuring a time when you are away from
the distraction of telephones or other people and create an "interview." It gives
nourishment to the speaker and helps the listener bypass defenses and resistance. Review important moments in that person's life, his career, his childhood
and look for Integrated Movements. The mood of an "interview" lets you bond
with the person, as you see, feel and hear the Integrated Movement. It is
relaxing and calming for both people. As the interviewer, you do not have to
comment or judge or reassure. Your role now virtually eliminates distracting
behaviors like annoyance, resentments, distracting glances, which get in the
way of the conversation. You just have to listen, watch and respond. You are
committed to the conversation.

Although it starts as an interview, the communication is really mutual. You
are both giving and receiving.

*"I used to become impatient or annoyed when my father and I talked. He
would become distracted or tired. I would slump down, sink into the chair,
collapsing my chest in dejection. I noticed this and changed my posture. It
helped."* It not only gives the speaker nourishment, but supports the listener to
bypass her own defenses and resistances.

Results Of Changing The Body Posture In Conversation

"I use Integrated Movement to assert myself in the family because my opinions and ideas are so different from theirs. If I don't, I find myself arguing or withdrawing."

"When I am with my father, I focus on his Integrated Movement as a way of giving him attention. Otherwise, he tends to be pushed into the background."

"Drawing attention to myself is something I have to work at."

"I must really prepare my posture and be sure to breathe, relax and stay buoyant like a balloon. If I shrink and shrivel up, the attention instantly leaves and I feel out on a limb."

"In my family, when I am synchronized with my mother and sister, I totally lose rapport with my husband and daughter. We seem to form an exclusive group which my husband and daughter do not know how to enter. I guess I need to work on the transition."

ROLE CHANGES AS OUR PARENTS AGE

If, as adults, we are caring for an aging parent, we may be surprised by our own negative feelings. Using Integrated Movement in these times can help keep a relationship from deteriorating beyond repair.

"I had made great progress with my mother. She was now eating regularly and willing to accept the delicious dinners I made. One night, when I was going to be out for dinner, I felt an implicit threat that she would not eat.

"'That's the thanks I get,' is what I wanted to say, or 'how dare you!' Then I thought about how important she is to me. I felt my concern. Luckily I caught my reaction in my posture and released it. I figured out what I needed to say: 'I'm delighted that you are eating now. I also have to know that you will eat when I am not here.' This became a way I could pull myself together and leave on a positive note, rather than in a state of conflict and ambivalence."

The caretaker must take of herself, physically and emotionally. She must check in with her own Integrated Movement state of being, catch any frustration in her posture, then use an Integrated Movement statement with sincerity and good feeling. Otherwise frustrated reactions may let a relationship seriously decline, even though the motivation for caregiving is love. We can fear synchronizing with the changes of age, as if it were a contagious disease. (Is age catching? If I understand and sympathize with this, will it happen to me?) The difference in energy level between the caregiver and receiver can promote antagonism. To avoid this, emphasize the natural empathy and attunement you feel. But be sure to plan physical recuperation to restore your own level of energy and vitality.

"Alice noticed that her relationship with her mother had changed. Her mother had helped her arrange babysitting and other household organizational details. Now her mother could no longer be relied on for this help. Alice missed this. In our discussion, Alice remembered a time when she spoke to her mother from her heart, discussing things that were very meaningful to her. At those times, Alice felt satisfied with the relationship. We had identified her Integrated Movement as she spoke. Realizing this, it was relatively easy for Alice to take charge of logistics and seek meaningful communication with her mother in other ways."

We mainly think of aging as skin wrinkling, getting flabby, losing strength or mental acuity. Astrologers have a more creative outlook. They look at life as cyclical. At age forty-five, life history appears to repeat its original cycle. The theory holds that we reexperience life in reverse. Could we feel a positive sense of completion and rediscovery in this? As certain faculties change, others are enhanced. When eyesight cannot pick up close details, we can gain a broader perspective. How many people view this as an enhancement rather than as an annoyance?

Communication patterns in aging are reminiscent of childhood. Think of the child's sing-song refrain as he asks for bubble gum. He sings a "bubble-gum" song to his mother, who ignores him, until he finally tugs at her sleeve and in a sharp voice breaks through with his request. The repetition involved in communicating with an aging parent is a little like this. The first signs of memory loss are shocking as one realizes that the shared memory bank is threatened. The repetitions can become infuriating. Your expectations have to change. Who is this? How will we relate? At this point the management of life becomes the main thing. We have to use whatever task is at hand as the vehicle of communication.

Suddenly all the previous disagreements and annoying patterns are much less important. They even become comforting. The very fact that one has to reduce worldly distractions to allow for communication becomes a positive simplification of life, a meditation. The elderly take on a kind of stillness. The inner calm may be a result of a hearing loss or of being left out socially. If approached and addressed, one often can see an immediate Integrated Movement.

The desire to just be and be still may increase. To stay vital and involved we have to cultivate our Integrated Movement as we age. We need to develop and maintain enjoyable activities which invest us with meaning and relevance;

demand new insights and stretch our creativity. As changes go on, we need to feel as loved and accepted as before. The love renews the desire to participate in the here-and-now and find expression in Integrated Movement.

SIBLINGS

By the nature of birth-order, siblings have totally different family roles. If only we had a handbook about these roles at birth, we might be able to avoid many alienating behaviors. If, for instance, the older sibling understood that she would feel like 'the responsible one' and her younger sibling would seem 'irresponsible,' the two of them might not become so committed to their roles. If there is a middle child and she understood that she is 'the mediator,' she might choose to take sides. If we all understood that we step into these roles 'accidently,' perhaps we could become more flexible with them.

"As I worked on my relationship with my sister, I learned that as a younger child, it was better for me to agree with her, supporting her authority and her role in the family. This generated rapport. Once I appreciated her point of view, she could respect mine. Initial disagreement only created a battle of roles."

Nowhere does past experience get in the way of a good relationship more easily than in families. Grudges become insurmountable crusades unless someone decides to start afresh.

In one family the relationship between three sisters deteriorated so much that communication between two of the sisters became all but impossible. Endless grievances had built up. Communication became colored with past emotions.

An opportunity for interaction arose: an invitation to dinner. I worked with Marie to create a "clean" response, one which related positively and directly to the event at hand and to nothing else. We reviewed the history of the relationship which was full of friction and misunderstandings. Finally, after Marie had expressed her anger and disappointments, she was able to respond convincingly to her sister's invitation. *"I would love to come, but not this time."* While the invitation was rejected, the way it was done created a positive response. No one felt fresh guilt and blame. As a matter of fact, a pleasant conversation followed. Each sister shared something positive about her life. Initially, this telephone call could have perpetuated rejection. Instead, cleaning out the volcano of Marie's feelings brought about a situation where positive communication could take place. This was a good beginning.

Life-size bronze sculpture titled "Hell, Time to go Fishing"

EIGHT

GETTING TO WORK

The movement qualities around friendship resemble a well-rehearsed dance, with its rhythmic regularity and synchrony of timing. Satisfying as this is, this quality is not essential for a productive working relationship, since it is possible to use postures, gestures and Integrated Movements effectively without this common unifying flow.

For instance, in a work setting we are more attentive to the outcome and product of communication than to the process, the feelings and moods. Business people can harmonize their postures, gestures and Integrated Movements to compliment their associate's and move a task forward even without personal affinity or a flowing mutuality. In other words, movement can create an environment to support the successful implementation of a task. Business associates may share a goal which they maintain in their posture, while keeping a distance through gestures and yet be open to suggestions or ideas expressed through Integrated Movement. A team like this would feel confident working together.

Complimentary strengths and differences in style are useful in collaborations, whereas similarity of personality, usually the basis of friendship, can be disastrous as working relationships. Friendship is a source of personal rejuvenation, where we let our hair down, "spill the beans," where we feel comfortable enough to present ourselves at our worst and be reminded of our best. But this freedom can strain a good working relationship where the goal is to accomplish a task. When mixing the two, we want to pay careful attention to boundaries and needs. The focus on Integrated Movement helps maintain the boundaries and definition of a good working relationship.

"A friend offered to cater a seminar I had organized. She arrived late one day. As we prepared, I said, 'It's okay that you were late today, but there are days

when it won't be. I'll be sure to tell you.' I felt comfortable and therefore went ahead directly with the Integrated Movement and statement. Her response was equal to it. Using an Integrated Movement she apologized, saying she would arrange her schedule so that it would not happen again. We both felt good."

Women establishing new businesses, exchanging expertise, or managing others for the first time, need clear boundaries. Men may have more established protocols and rituals, but will find these principles helpful reminders.

- ❖ Realize when you have been asked for support beyond the agreement. Decide whether you really wish to exceed this boundary.
- ❖ Do not act out of emotion. An emotional outburst can be interpreted as jealousy, insecurity or an unrelated response echoing another situation. It is not the best way to return to the work.
- ❖ Reestablish the boundaries in a polite way. *"Your idea sounds very interesting; I wish you a lot of success."* Shift your posture to show a change in topic as you make this acknowledgment.
- ❖ Use an Integrated Movement as you return to the task at hand. *"How is my project coming along? Have you sent the letters to the publishers?"*

A successful manager must be able to assert authority when behavior is unacceptable.

- ❖ Know your own limits.
- ❖ Posture will help you defend your position.
- ❖ Spell out the details of your plan with clear gestures.
- ❖ Request specific action.
- ❖ Use Integrated Movement so that you do not encourage defensive behavior.

A friend spoke to me about a problem she was having: *"My foreman hired an assistant to work for him, with my approval. But the assistant was interfering with the decisions and planning. I wanted a change. My first reaction was emotional: 'he's taking advantage of me.'* Recognizing this, I shifted to a more total view of the economics of the situation. Using an Integrated Movement, I said to the foreman: *"You are very valuable to me. Please keep careful records of your assistant. How long will it take for him to finish what he is working on now because I can't afford him very much longer."*

Analysis Of The Communication:

1. You did a great job. (Posture, the position you are taking.)
2. Your assistant was good too. (Posture, respecting his judgment.)
3. I have to focus on expenses more carefully now. (Gesture, sharing information.)
4. I would like to do without him after this project. Can you manage that? (Integrated Movement, expression of need.)

In some instances, you may choose to explain your shift of choice: *"I felt I could help your friend and had enough work for you both. Now circumstances have changed. I need to return to working with you alone."* You might chose one or the other approach depending on the circumstances. Once you arrive at your Integrated Movement statement and feel confident, you can negotiate easily.

If you become unsure of yourself, complications and tangles may creep back into your thought process along with postures and gestures. Reinforce your solution as best you can by writing it down or telling it to someone else, so that you hear it and feel it again. Use an image which will help you recreate the change you have made. Eventually the behavior will become second-nature.

POSITIONING YOURSELF FOR SUCCESS

If you find yourself responding negatively to every suggestion or idea made at a meeting, it is a sign you have found your way into a posture. Analyze the ingredients of your reaction. Be honest about your attitude, your posture. Once your intentions are clear, take positive steps.

State the facts using gestures: *"I am stating my objections because I am really fed up."* The level of honesty you are asking of yourself may well materialize in an Integrated Movement. This will pull things together nicely for you and give you the group's attention. By using this approach, you may gain respect or authority.

In most business situations you have to evoke your own Integrated Movement and then make a case for it. Your emotions, feelings, thoughts and opinions have to become a bridge to action. With practice you will become very efficient at finding Integrated Movement solutions.

Obstacles and frustrations are an opportunity for Integrated Movement. Each time you meet an obstacle or frustration, think: *"how can I get through this? What do I want to do? Where is my energy really invested? What do I need so that I can be enthusiastic?"* When you think this way, you can become highly motivated.

Picture what you do want, define a plan, and start the creative process. Look at the benefits for you. Look at the benefits for others. Let your emotional intensity come through your words and body as an Integrated Movement. The body involvement will spring from the thought process and vice versa.

Do not anticipate a negative response and shrivel up. Your Integrated Movement will vanish. Take advantage of your intense feelings to articulate your motivation and make things clear. Even if your goal is not achieved, you will have made a powerful impression which will probably gain recognition for you. Speaking out convincingly begins to establish your role as leader.

For instance, suppose your director is against a mini-conference because she thinks there isn't time to plan it and it will cost too much money. Good ideas are often postponed indefinitely. You can confront delaying tactics directly so that you can address the objections. Ask: *"If I can satisfy these objections can I go ahead?"* If the answer is yes, then you have the motivation to solve the problems.

Motivation flags if we feel undermined or over-controlled. Constant supervision can hinder your motivation. Too many rules may create lack of interest. *"We were enjoying the task of creating a new promotion when suddenly, the director began imposing her ideas on us. The director saw our energy visibly dissolve and so withdrew the limitations she was imposing."*

Presenting an idea with Integrated Movement needs preparation:

1. Step back and see the situation as a whole. Think through the benefits to you, to others, and all possible objections.

2. Know your goal thoroughly and be prepared to work for it.

3. Let the intensity of your motivation build.

4. Be flexible with details and consider other people's ideas as much as possible so that they feel part of the process. Avoid 'take it or leave it' solutions.

BEING A "SELF-STARTER"

Settling down to work involves different rituals for each of us. Some straighten the desk, some make a list. We physically position ourselves for the task. When ideas are flowing and things are happening, we feel the momentum and a sense of success. When we have to start up from scratch, there is much more resistance. Newton's laws of perpetual motion apply here too. Details of office organization, planning ahead, figuring out a budget are all creative activities. Although all tasks have a degree of drudgery, they can be imbued with investment and involvement with questions like:

What are the potential rewards of this work?

What skills will I have when I am done?

What purpose is this serving?

The answers allow our thought and body to become reintegrated, capable of rekindling Integrated Movement and reminding us of what is most nourishing in the work we are doing. This kind of concentration on a task makes it meaningful.

IMPROVING WORKING RELATIONSHIPS

Joan was so unhappy at work and with one colleague in particular, that she was considering leaving her job. She was familiar with Integrated Movement and she knew she was deliberately not using it. By making this choice, she also chose not to express herself, not to be vulnerable or honest in dealing with her colleague.

My role was to watch, listen and describe postures. Joan was aware that she was exacerbating the problem by her postures. *"I start our conversations by not listening. Instead I think, 'I don't like what you are doing. You are unreasonable, but you walk around criticizing us. I will not cooperate."* These were the postures she described. Then she had a personal revelation: *"I should say what is on my mind."* In order to be able to, she began thinking:

What's bothering me?

How am I perpetuating the problem?

What do I really want to say?

How can I be honest in a professional way?

At the next business meeting, Joan was able to confront her colleague directly. She finally spoke with passion and things began moving in a better direction.

We are constantly using these strategies. Observing a colleague talking on the telephone, I confirmed the true intent and quality of the interaction by watching her postures, gestures and Integrated Movement. I knew she had three difficult issues to resolve in her discussion. The description of what I saw follows:

E: *"You used gestures of concern and understanding. You did not assume a counter-posture, even though it was obvious you were getting resistance.*

"You used calming gestures. You had a posture of consideration and authority, arms folded as you leaned to the side. Your personal self-touch gestures seemed to keep you involved while you were listening. Then, you shifted your weight to the other foot. It was as if to say, lets shift to the next topic. With a big Integrated Movement, you requested a change in a hotel reservation. The rest you managed very well with gestures."

P: *(Describing her own view of the telephone conversation.) "She spoke from an abrupt, business-like posture. There was no leeway for pleasantries. Do you think my reassuring gestures helped make my point more effectively?"*

E: *"Yes. You did find common ground, though it never seemed like a warm, friendly exchange. But you got the task done. You each seemed to express yourselves clearly, were heard, and accomplished the necessary changes. It was quite efficient."*

NEGOTIATIONS

Every dialogue is a negotiation. Each time two bodies meet to talk, they negotiate the space, the timing, the content of the discussion. Most negotiations slip by without much attention focused on them because they happen within our natural repertory of movement and words. Negotiations are a way of resolving or avoiding conflict as well as a way of sharing, exchanging and changing ideas.

Each time we make an appointment to discuss an issue, we establish a more formal negotiation. Some negotiations, like those between Heads of State, are so formal that everyone must stay in their stated postures. The real negotiation may happen through a third party or behind closed doors. Too much is at stake to entrust it to the parties immediately concerned. With each round of discussion, some posture is needed to state the conditions, some gestures are needed to describe the issues and some trial solutions must be attempted with Integrated Movement.

As a negotiation gets underway, people demonstrate their position by their posture. One cannot have a meaningful negotiation without being aware of each other's position. Temporarily leaving a posture, then returning to it, adds support and emphasis. It is the job of gestures to iron out differences. Using gestures which are consistent to the meaning of a posture, helps maintain a position and renew it, rather than allowing it to become rigid. Then, Integrated Movement seals the deal.

GROUPS

Groups are like clouds, constantly changing formation; aggregating, condensing, reducing, expanding. Within any given group, people form clusters, shift, change. As postures and attitudes change, moods can change from light and buoyant to dark and threatening; from chaotic to controlled, from frantic to serene. The group encompasses all the individuals and the spaces between them. Thus the 'negative' space surrounding each individual and each cluster is part of the group and subject to movement dynamics and changes in form.

A group has its own postures, gestures and Integrated Movements which resound through it like air waves. Our power in groups is actually so great it intimidates some of us and we withdraw into our individuality. Being part of a group means recognizing our similarity to other members as well as our distinct roles.

Our sense of our own individuality is a function of our cultural and family group. Groups of one type or another are an ever-present aspect of life. My goal is to help each of us bring our individuality back to the group, with an understanding of the life and movement of the group itself and our particular function in it.

When a group is of one mind, because of beliefs or a shared experience, individuals assume a similarity of posture. The group members seem invisibly bound together. They move with a sense of togetherness, like folk dancers or the players in a string quartet. The Sontac Philippine war dance, Hasidic male dancers at a wedding, athletes in a basketball game: all of these show the same cohesion. The movement solidifies the group and conveys compelling and powerful feelings. Group cohesion is an essential ingredient for maintaining culture. Of course the hypnotic power of a group can be misused in the extreme when people suppress their individual wisdom and succumb to madmen or power-hungry leaders.

AN INTEGRATED GROUP

The postures, gestures, and Integrated movements in a healthy group are like those of an individual. The efficient gestures will handle tasks and details; the postures will maintain group purpose and mission; the Integrated Movement will unify the group action. The balance and interplay of all three will keep the group healthy and effective. If the group cannot cohere, it is in trouble.

If its attitudes are stuck and rigid, it is in trouble. If it can never break apart and piece itself together, it is in trouble. When a group is flexible enough to recognize and use each member's potential, it is inspiring and beautiful to watch.

ESTABLISHING A GROUP

In a workshop of sixty people, I asked all those who were students to raise their hands. When they did, it became apparent that the students were all sitting against the back wall. Everyone was surprised and we all laughed. The message was clear.

Groupings are based on natural and learned affinities. In an experiment with couple formations, strangers paired off to spend time focusing on each other, silently at first. Each looked at the other in order to establish similarities or points of appreciation. They were asked to become as receptive as possible to the other person. Another group established rapport by mirroring each other's movement.

Both ways, pair bonding was established. I then asked some pairs to separate and join other pairs. Gestures proliferated at first. In some cases, postures were eventually shared and the new person was accepted. In other groups, the original pair remained connected, but the new individual remained outside, sometimes rejected, sometimes dominating, but nevertheless, outside.

In a subsequent exercise, each pair joined another pair. The pair seemed to transfer its harmony to the new group. Each pair had to give up part of its symmetry to establish a new whole but it was clearly an easier adjustment. The separate groups continued joining. By the time the whole group was reunited, there was a strong basis for sharing, coming from the adjustments in postures and gestures which were made.

Powerful perceptions and the movement they engender continuously influence our formation of groups. These structures can be influenced, to some degree, through awareness. For example, pair bonding eases social interactions. A couple sharing each other's support, has an easier time in a group. The first unit is already formed and seeks other similar units. In a group, people look for familiar faces and gravitate toward them. If someone is alone, he or she looks for someone else in that situation. Each might acknowledge the other and begin a communication centered around something shared, possibly the common fact of each not being in a pair.

We can influence our experiences in a group by consciously recreating what happens in optimal circumstances. When we watch someone we like, we automatically make pleasant associations and generate positive feelings. We relax, breathe more deeply and generally feel good. A bond is created. This can take place in a fleeting moment with no real awareness that it is happening. We can create this receptive state by choice. If this leads to a conversation, we would then find ourselves creating symmetrical or complementary postures, sculpting ourselves into a unit. The cohesion of the unit will encourage the trust needed to share meaningful aspects of ourselves in Integrated Movements, and a bond is deepened.

A group structure is fragile. Alliances change, alienation can happen. When someone in a group really bothers us, instead of becoming entangled in the negative qualities, we can create positive ones, by associating the person with a pleasant memory or thought. Although this does not necessarily give you the tools for working out long-term problems, it is an effective way of being open to a new point of view.

EFFECTING CHANGE

A group can get locked into a pattern that no one likes, yet feel unable to change it. People in groups often cannot articulate their needs. They think they are alone with that need, when in fact, they may represent a large part of the group.

We absorb group postures and play into them. (Everyone is interrupting, we interrupt to say, 'stop interrupting.') Group movement is contagious and so is group behavior.

The nature and evolution of groups follows definite patterns. The group will always reflect its issues in its posture. Using secrecy to accomplish one's goals will translate into secrecy in the way group members relate to each other. If you take time to sense the mood or experience of the group, you can begin to address the need for change. As you do this, you are developing a sensitivity to the "mind" of the group, a sensitivity which lets you flow with the moving, changing group quality, with its conditional truths. Noticing the mind of the group lets you affect it because it gives you choices. However, if the group is in an antagonistic posture, it may reject your good ideas and block action.

Address the group posture itself. Assume an appropriately conciliatory posture so that you are not setting yourself up in opposition to the group. (Mirror the group posture.) *"We seem to be critical of every suggestion. Perhaps we are really unhappy with the status of things. What can we do about it?"* For a moment you encourage the group to reflect on itself and possibly move to a more productive posture. Even in an informal group of friends, this may be a handy technique: imagine everyone advising one person simultaneously. Say: *"We are all giving advice,"* (articulating the group posture). Then, address the person with a gesture or Integrated Movement, asking: *"Is this what you need now?"*

It is hard for one person to have the presence of mind to detach from the group and observe it and then to be willing to stand out from the group and be the focus of its energy. Perhaps this is why a feeling of immobility often seems to overtake us in a group, almost as if our movement patterns have chained us to silence. It is a risk not to be taken lightly, because when we successfully shift the group mind, the group may then look to us for leadership.

CHANGING THE GROUP MIND

In a supportive group, you will find yourself in a harmonious posture with others without even realizing it. It will be easy to find the group posture, feel it, show you understand, then proceed with your approach. Changing the group mind is different.

It is not difficult to see the difference between an exhausted or disinterested group and one that is eager and ready to work. As the leader, it is your job to help the group shift. One way is through movement. I usually ask a group to make a semi-circle for a presentation. This immediately shifts their attitude and they begin to wonder what to expect.

To successfully lead a group, an awareness of the group mind is obviously very important. Ignoring the group posture can be disaster for a leader. Since a group posture is very hard to change, use the same skills you developed to release an individual posture: identify it, match it, move out of it with an Integrated Movement.

In an experiment, Rob tried to get five people who were in a resistant state to support the direction of the organization. At first he ignored their posture. He got nowhere. He was as sincere as possible and used his Integrated Movement persuasively, but they continued to maintain their negative attitude and he was ineffective. Next, he joined them. He first had to become one of them to understand their point of view. Then, from a position of trust, he could influence their attitude. As we found with individuals, it is more effective to join the posture as a first step to change.

This next situation required the leader to generate a posture as powerful as the group's in order to shift the group mind.

P: *"The group was posturing confusion, then rebellion, then mutiny!"*

E: *"What did you do?"*

P: *"I had to match their posture. I pulled myself up to my full height, and said: 'don't argue with me.' I assumed my authority as teacher. An Integrated*

Movement would have been too honest and revealing. In their posture, it would have aggravated the situation. I was one, they were twelve. Why should one Integrated Movement convince them all? Anyway, my authority was being threatened.

"The group had become critical when they had to be receptive to learning new concepts. From my posture of authority, I recreated a receptive state, using meditation. Then I could go back to being honest with them and use Integrated Movement. I pulled them together with a posture, changed the group 'mind,' then went back to teaching.

"I have noticed that people posture a lot more when they are insecure. A bit of confusion, some scattered gestures, and the whole group disintegrates. When you are secure, you can tolerate a few moments of not knowing."

One last example shows an effective change from a calm meeting to a more emotional, volatile one.

"At one of our annual professional meetings, a very hot political issue came up. The leader chose to deal with it in a cool, gestural way. This worked for a while until the group's collective emotions exploded! It turned out to be a relief. It let the group go through a lot of heated arguments freely as preparation for truly resolving the issue satisfactorily. It was surprisingly efficient."

FINDING YOUR INDIVIDUAL VOICE

The stronger the bond between individuals in the group, the stronger the sense of group. Each role in a group has its function and affects the whole decision-making process.

Decision-making in a group is not a personal affair but requires approval, support, involvement of others. One decision bears on another and needs to be communicated. The process is complex. In an organization, all effort is ultimately a reflection of the group. Even when an individual is singled out for praise, the whole organization benefits. Finding your voice in a group strengthens the potential and the outcome of group action. This does not mean each individual has to compete for attention. It means each person must take responsibility for her role in the group. The role may be consistent or it may change from meeting to meeting or from group to group.

Groups are strong because of the contributions of each member. It is helpful to clearly identify these individual strengths, and to be able to call upon them when addressing specific goals. By listening carefully to each contribution, the interaction will stay mobile and alive. Maintaining a sense of individuality and participating productively in a group is a momentous task for those raised in the western culture. Here is a way to begin to identify the role you play.

Your role in the group will be influenced by several choices you make as you enter the room: where you go, the position you take in relation to other people, even the way you feel about your choices. To make the most of your active group contribution, you also want to be aware of the attitude and posture you assume when you join the group.

Evaluate your comfort level through your posture. Decide if you need to move. If so, do. Get some water, or choose a different chair. Reflect on the reasons why you were or were not comfortable in the first place. Notice how your choices affect your role in the group. If they have worked well for you, good. If not, be sure to change them next time.

DISCOVERING YOUR IDEAL GROUP

In a group, we can set up a harmonious working atmosphere by having each person articulate his needs. In this way, the group can accommodate and be responsive to many of them. Conversely, if we try to make the group fit our personal needs, we end up struggling against it and can lock ourselves into positions.

If we are uncomfortable or unappreciated in a group, we tend to blame the group or the leader. We think that our personal needs are right and other needs are wrong. We assume that our way is better and wonder why others are so ignorant, inept, stubborn.

In a workshop, we discovered how personal needs can be accommodated in a group.

"I was amazed that I could function in a group that felt so different from my ideal. People came and went at random in this group, going off by themselves to do individual tasks. I did too. When I wanted support, I found someone to assist me. I realized that I was quite happy with this structure."

"I feel a group should encourage individual development. The group becomes stronger in the long run."

"Harry likes people to work independently and then share the result of their work. I thought this would create overlapping effort and be impossible to coordinate. In fact we were all eager to hear what the others had done. Some ideas were discarded, but the end result was better for the depth of exploration we had."

"The exercise taught me that we could be flexible and participate in each other's experience. It felt satisfying. We accepted each other's differences instead of battling it out in the group."

Once you know it is possible to satisfy different needs in a group and have identified your own, you can more easily create groups to serve these needs.

MAKING YOUR NEEDS KNOWN

Talk about the group. What does it want? What is expected? (Attendance, involvement, concern.)

What do I need the group to know about me? (I love to come up with extraneous ideas; I like change for its own sake.)

What kinds of things can I give this group? (Stability, experience, support.)

What do I need from the group? (Freedom to walk around in the middle of a meeting.)

What agreements can we make to allow for each other's needs? (You give us a signal if it gets too boisterous.)

In Practice

"The whole group was in agreement except me. I did not like the proposal. Although I did not want to be disruptive, I felt that my concerns were serious. I broke away from the group to privately discuss my objection with a colleague. She assured me the idea was valid and explained why. I agreed. Because I had practiced exercising my need in a group, I felt free to create this private discussion, then return to the group."

A good working group may not always look smooth, calm and efficient. There can be tension, shouting, pushing and pulling to generate new ideas and decisions. If there is underlying good-will, spontaneity and intensity tends to unify people. Each success builds confidence and trust for the next time.

GROUP PREJUDICE

Groups, by their very nature, are exclusive. There will be those who "belong" and those who don't. People are comfortable with others when they share common beliefs, customs and movement patterns. So naturally, those who don't conform seem alien and strange. Prejudice, therefore, is a natural consequence of groups.

The nature of prejudice is a dualistic view of the world. If one group is inferior, then the other must be superior. In this thinking, each group must protect itself from the other; each group builds itself by having scorn for others.

If groups are facing limited resources, low status, legal repression, political powerlessness or oppression, they have the benefit of a unified force to act, and the danger of taking out their frustrations on each other. They have their own helpless postures to mirror and the temptation to oppress others in order to gain a sense of power. Sharing common problems will be useful for a while to help activate the energy to act. Dissatisfaction with the status quo will also generate energy. But at some point, someone has to lead the way to productive action.

The minority group must strengthen its identity and project this positive image. The group must become known for its strengths, its self-respect and its internal power. (Strength from within commands respect from without.) This will attract larger, more powerful group support. Until the posture is matched, the controlling group has no reason to pay attention to the minority group. Some alignment of postures is necessary for negotiation to take place. Each group can find its own power by making the very attributes which distinguish it as "different" into its assets. To simply accept external criteria would mean learning through another culture's postures and gestures. It would be artificial and disembodied. The less dominant group would sacrifice its identity in the process.

In the extreme, where oppression is entrenched legally, politically or economically, revolution may be necessary. But in the more subtle kind of hierarchy, the minority opinion can take the grass-roots approach to change through personal responsibility and action. The dominant culture will eventually integrate the minority as the other culture demonstrates tangible benefits.

Instances where this has happened are:

The State of Israel. By forming the state of Israel, Jewish people asserted their own identity. They created a cohesive force and proved themselves against impressive odds.

The Black Power Movement. Blacks gained respect for the very cultural differences that had enslaved them. Their identity needed strengthening from within to counteract decades of abuse.

The Women's Liberation Movement. Critics described women who participated as "unfeminine," and charged that they risked losing the preferred status of mother and nurturer. Nonsense. The Movement created a new awareness of the multiple capabilities of women, and resulted in the Equal Rights Amendment.

The group asserting itself must meet the power group on an equal footing, with strong postures and gestures. From this sense of strength, new skills and new behaviors can be learned in order to make comfortable bridges between groups.

OVERCOMING GROUP PREJUDICE

The force of prejudice is mitigated by individual understanding. Frozen mental attitudes and body defenses change when we take the opportunity to establish rapport with an individual who belongs to the group in disfavor.

"My prejudice against Germans for their role in World War II made it difficult for me to relate to German students. I had a chance to explore my mistrust of Germans with a colleague who was partially of German heritage. The personal history of what the war was like for her grandparents, and how contemporary Germans themselves feel about the Holocaust issue, was most helpful. My inability to address the subject before maintained my attitude. I realized I could learn more by asking questions and gaining understanding than by holding on to my posture.

"As individuals, we moved from postures to Integrated Movements. We needed sympathy and understanding and were able to give them to each other. We listened and responded with deep feeling. Later, we both acknowledged a great sense of healing."

Here is a less dramatic situation, but a common one for young groups who are establishing standards and criteria for membership. John was a new member in a group which April had founded. April, offended by the regulations which were now being imposed on her, would no longer associate with the group. John wished to address these issues with her. He found April very unreceptive.

John ingratiated himself by his respectful manner and by mirroring April's postures. She knew that he was aware of her attitudes and was prepared to listen. When April accepted him as an individual, she responded with Integrated Movement and became more comfortable. They analyzed their movement:

A: *"I felt my upper body was open even though I was turning away. He used a big, engaging Integrated Movement. I followed with one. My purpose was strictly to pull myself together. All of a sudden, he waved at me. I asked why he did that gesture."*

J: *"April had excluded me. The gesture was my way of saying, 'I'm here'."*

A: *"That worked for me."*

J: *"Then I did an Integrated Movement towards April and she nodded her head."*

A: *"I felt myself about to get involved in old battles. His close attention to my position and his Integrated Movement gave me the chance to see him as a person in his own right, and not as a defender of the group. I wonder now, if it would have been easier if I had not been in a posture? I was afraid that if I were natural, I would have gotten into my Integrated Movement, shared more than was appropriate and more than I wanted to feel.*

"I actually learned how much maintaining this posture was costing me. It was time for me to accept the situation without so much anger."

GROUP PROCESS

Group process is a specific time set aside for a group to study itself. A leader is usually chosen who watches and reflects what is happening to the group. Nothing goes unnoticed. Everything now becomes meaningful because everything is symbolic of the group process. It is a time of heightened awareness and sensitivity, like watching the protoplasm of a cell under a microscope. For example: you might see four people with their legs stretched out and crossed; two are leaning on their elbows; three are leaning away from the circle with angulated bodies. At once, the group starts to look like petals of a flower. Then it shifts and changes for no apparent reason other than underlying thought patterns, recording temporary links and affiliations to someone of a similar mind. What seems random, has pattern.

There are moments when the group becomes still with no distracting gestures; times when everyone is caught up in one scattering of chaotic little individual movements, grooming gestures, fixing socks, touching hair. There is a kind of dispersion. Why at that moment? What was said? Who spoke? Subgroupings of people in similar postures appear. New alignments are made. Everyone becomes collected until the next moment of focus. When you watch the group in this way you notice and become part of the botanical evolution of the group.

If you are part of a group and wish to try some group process methods, here are some suggestions:

❖ Choose a topic: Where are we in our evolution as a group? What are our greatest problems? Goals? Needs? What issues hinder our effectiveness?

❖ Sit quietly and wait for someone to respond.

In the discussion, make sure that each person responds and that no one person dominates. A good session can redirect a group into a more positive focus. It can solidify a group. It can give the group definition and clarity about itself and its tasks. Everyone sees the anatomy of the group, how it functions, its process and content, its problems and strengths. A behavior pattern which was likely to remain unchanged for the course of the group life often changes after being addressed in a group session.

FLEXIBLE LEADERSHIP

Groups are fertile ground for the development of leadership qualities. In its broadest definition, leadership is the response of the group to the speaker. A leader is not only the person in charge, but a person who creates change in the group. A leader may temporarily refocus the group in some way. Even one statement which shifts the group from hostile to supportive is a moment of leadership.

Leadership is the act of taking responsibility for saying and doing what is truly important. By speaking up, one initiates a chain of action which has consequences. Understandably, it's a risk many people shy away from. By now though, you realize that Integrated Movement is about that part of yourself that is willing to take a risk.

What are the risks? You could be ineffective. You could create a different effect than you had intended. You could be very effective and now responsible for change. As long as you are prepared for each of these possibilities, your risk is a calculated one.

You will be more likely to risk group leadership if you understand and are comfortable with your personal leadership tendencies. To gain this comfort, you want to understand your own thoughts and feelings and have a good grasp on the solution. As you speak, you will be most effective if your Integrated Movement is consistent with your attitude, your posture. Avoid any secondary impressions or gestures which could dilute the effect of your statement. If you seem to act superior, bullying or timid, people may react to the posture and never experience the Integrated Movement.

The role you play in a group may be different from your leadership role. Your role in a group is about the piece of behavior which always seems to fall to you. It is the initiative you take as one member, satisfying your own need. Offering a suggestion or having an idea is not the same as taking the reins and asking the group to follow you in a new direction. This obviously takes a different conviction on your part and a different level of intensity. If you play a dominant role in the group, you may be invited to lead. If you have a very clear sense of what the group should do, your leadership inclinations may be frustrated. You may want to support the current efforts of the group before offering your ideas. This will prepare you for gaining support when you need it to lead the group effectively.

SECOND-LEVEL LEADERSHIP

If a group wants a leader it must offer support. Otherwise the leader is like the king in *The Little Prince* who "ordered" people to do exactly what they wanted to do. A leader can only go as far as the people around him will allow, unless, of course, he becomes a dictator. This is when a second level of leadership is necessary. The best way to create leadership is through teamwork. People feel valued and important when they are supporting a leader. At crucial moments, someone often stands out from the group and assists it. Here are the ways I have noticed that this happens. Look for these shifts in your next group experience.

The Action Leader

This leader energizes action. She takes the ball once it has started rolling and helps get results. A suggestion is made to have a strategic planning retreat. She offers to locate the best facility. By moving into commitment and implementing the decision, she rids the group of hesitation and begins generating enthusiasm and action. The action leader can help move masses of people, calmly and comfortably. She organizes tasks and provides needed skills to see projects through. She focuses the group on the goal.

The Supporting Leader

This leader helps the group cohere and act. He reminds the group of its purpose and keeps the group on track while supporting the leader. He can sustain the strength of the leader while smoothing out conflicts. Temporary disagreements do not fester and erupt into major rebellions. The supporting leader keeps priorities straight, keeps competitiveness from destroying the group. As an able spokesperson, he can articulate the leader's strengths and focus the group's attention on the leader.

The Process Leader

This leader maintains some distance from the group in order to observe its methods and focus the group's attention on a need for change, a change in procedure or approach. This person watches the "comfort level" in the group and asks for adjustments she perceives as necessary. She keeps the leader in touch with the group needs. The Process Leader focuses on the group dynamic.

In fact, all three secondary leaders are supporting the official leader in a team effort of assisting and facilitating action. Too often we view the leader as the sole person responsible for the group, but the group is also responsible for the effectiveness of the leader.

A leader's responsibility is to understand an issue, find a solution, present it fully and experience the effect on the group. Your reaction to the following descriptions will tell you which leadership styles you like and can work with and which you find frustrating. Think about which of these types of leaders are most like you and what kind of support each would need.

Leader 1. Knows the goal, sees the steps clearly and defines the action needed to accomplish it. He creates a strategy based on analysis; recommends it with confidence and makes it easy for the group to act.

Leader 2. Synthesizes the issues and gives a good status report. She expects the group to provide the expertise and set a new direction. Structure must be clearly defined before action is taken. Careful attention is given to rules and regulations. This leader might make procedural suggestions or wish to diagram the concepts.

Leader 3. This is the "founding father." He shares his experience and motivates by example. He provides historical continuity and a loving focus. This leader generates feeling by sharing the joys and sadness of his early experiences. He does not have to create a vision or mission, only respect for the struggle. His total involvement is persuasive.

Leader 4. This leader is a teacher. The group learns by example. Their leader's statements are philosophical, even enigmatic. The mere presence of this type of leader draws a group and can catalyze action. The group members feel part of an elite organization.

Leader 5. This leader is super-sensitive to the group. She runs things by popular consent and works hard to know what is on everyone's mind.

Leader 6. This leadership style is extremely efficient, with no room for emotional reactions. The leader maintains order and calm at all cost. She controls outcome with information. Formality is the prevailing atmosphere. (Here, gestures may be very helpful to get things done efficiently with a minimum of emotion.) Central commitment must remain strong or the group may lose motivation.

Leader 7. This person leads by charisma, displaying a contagious sense of purpose. He generates feeling and popular opinion invariably follows him. He must be aware that commitment to ideas without practical implementation can also lead to fragmentation.

Leader 8. This leader leads by title. He can award titles, tasks and favors. He must establish the boundaries and territory within which the group functions. Projecting glamour and earning the respect of the group is his main job. He has many constraints and is not free to shift roles as readily as the other leaders.

Some physical change happens when one is motivated to lead. If you feel exasperated, you may find yourself absorbed in gestures. Thoughts of anger, blame, isolation may lead to a large shift of posture. This tells you that a big change is necessary. Observe your movement and track your thoughts. Clarify them. Watch the group and see if their reaction matches yours. Judge the timing and prepare to act with a clear Integrated Movement and statement. Observe your effect on the group. Ask the group if it shares your reaction.

By gaining confidence in your style, you will allow more Integrated Movement expression. It will become a signature. Your need for support as a leader and your supporting role as a group member will become more obvious. You will think about what you need and what the group needs. It will become easier for you to ask for support or offer leadership in a comfortable, full-bodied, integrated way.

POLITICAL LEADERS

In America, our political leaders come from the economic and intellectual elite, for the most part. Yet they present themselves as "mortal" human beings, sharing concerns of the common man. More and more we require leaders who respond directly to the needs of the people; leaders who demonstrate conviction and trust, verbally and physically.

The public gives high scores to a candidate who expresses himself with conviction and lets it show in his body. Then they really know where he stands and what he thinks. For instance, both vice presidential candidates in 1984, Ferraro and Bush, showed equal amounts of Integrated Movement, over different topics and in different ways. The next morning, the newspapers corroborated our observations of equal investment by calling the debate a draw.

Comparing Reagan and Mondale in the same election, we saw Reagan as regal, master of the gracious gesture and munificent posture. He relied on charm rather than sincerity. He had trouble managing the facts, therefore had a hard time expressing his concerns fully.

Mondale, lacking the skills of posture and gesture, had to rely on sincerity and vulnerability. He demonstrated these in extemporaneous moments, when he spoke directly to Reagan, disarming and flustering him. In the debate, that action won Mondale lots of points with the public.

In 1992, Clinton showed warmth and empathy to the public by moving away from the podium, walking towards the audience and addressing specific people with the concern of a friend. Bush, on the other hand, was disconcerted when asked how the recession affected him personally. He stayed still, made no gesture, and had trouble relating to the question.

Of course, most people are not analyzing Integrated Movement. They form impressions. Knowledge of the significance of Integrated Movement, however, lets us evaluate a candidate's true involvement in vital issues. On camera, we can look for physical movement which either validates or negates our impression. Integrated Movement will tell us just how much a candidate is willing to put behind his words. This knowledge should help us see through political posturing, pretensions, and let us know what is really behind our leader's words. [1]

E: *"Suppose we showed the debaters what worked, and said,'is this what you think about this issue? Because this is how it is coming across.' And the politician said; 'you're right. Something is keeping me from a whole-hearted expression. I'd better work on that.' They would have to present a more thorough understanding of the issue to really be convincing and the voters would have much more information in making a decision."*

P: *"Then politicians wouldn't have to be actors. But they would have to practice presenting their conviction to huge crowds; actually, the whole world."*

E: *"If you are a serious man, don't try to smile a lot. Tell us you are serious. That's what gives us confidence in you. Politics is no laughing matter."*

P: *"We want to know what our politicians really think about the issues. It's not about getting better at putting across what someone else writes. It's about finding their own deep motivation and truth."*

NINE

THE BODY

Your body is a living, breathing, complex combination of chemical interactions and physical forces all humming along, maintaining your health and being a diligent servant. You owe it to yourself to take care of this body and listen to its wonderful rhythms and pulses. Make friends with its accomplishments, even its ailments, as you influence them with knowledge and gentle attention.

This chapter will help you become more familiar with your own skills, tensions or blocks in the sports and exercises you do. A study of gestures, postures and Integrated Movements will enhance the enjoyment you already get from your exercise activities.

Gestures are a means of stimulating circulation, differentiating joint articulations and preparing specific muscle groups for action. Postures stretch the body and elongate tired or sore muscles, thereby releasing tension and restoring resilience. By concentrating on postures and gestures in a warm-up, you are consciously avoiding stress or strain in specific parts of the body, making sure each one has what it needs. By using Integrated Movement you are preparing a totally coordinated effort.

You don't have to be an expert in a sport to know that something is interfering with the smooth process of action. You are perceiving the lack of integration.

A swimmer reported that when her mind was focused on the movement of her body in the water she could swim the length of a pool in seven strokes. When her mind wandered, it took nine. The sense of total investment and concentration on the Integrated Movement brought her greater efficiency.

As you pay attention to Integrated Movement, you emphasize the moment when the whole body lets go to action. The mind is focused on the feeling and experience rather than on the goal. You stay present in the moment. A way to capture this experience of exhilarated physical performance is to identify the image or metaphor you feel at that moment: sailing through space, a speeding comet, sculpting shapes in the snow. Then you can use the image to recreate the satisfying movement experience instead of muscling your way through.

A SKIER

Alex, an expert ski instructor, showed Integrated Movement as he "skied" down a grassy slope. He explained the process. *"You create a nice, slow sine wave as you shift all your weight to the uphill ski, flattening it, letting it turn downhill then beginning the process again as you enter the fall line.*

"You think about bringing your whole body forward as you follow through. You accelerate, then get a really good rebound. You feel like you are falling down the hill.

"You can also skate straight down the hill to get the acceleration. It's kind of intimidating so you think of skating to someone. You pretend that you have a line attached from your belly button to that person. It's a total commitment."

Listening to Alex, it is clear that he is integrating his movement even when he talks about skiing. Athletes find a way to use their Integrated Movement whether or not they give it a name.

YOUR EXERCISE REGIME

Let's consider your current exercise methods and analyze them. Do you bicycle? Where do you think your Integrated Movement could be? Perhaps on the push of the pedal or, if you have toe straps, on the pull up? Maybe you integrate more on the release, or in the breath of recuperation after the exertion. Experience the moment when your whole body supports a specific part of the action. You may want to notice too, where your body is tightening and holding for the sake of another part. Is this creating strain?

Do you jog? The next time you are out jogging, catch the moment when everything feels consistent and continuous throughout your whole body. Is it the strong push into the ground, or the light moment in the air? Is it the convex moment when the torso arches ahead? If you are not sure, start by looking for gestures. Notice foot gestures, how the lower leg swings forward. Notice the arm gestures. The point where one of these gestures links up with the rest of them is your Integrated Moment.

Seeking an Integrated Movement will put the emphasis in the right place and may result in a shift of attitude allowing the body a more unified, pleasurable experience. If you find one, you are probably enjoying what you are doing.

If you cannot find an Integrated Movement in the exercise you do, the whole process may be a series of gestures. You may want to change.

Exercise regimes have much to offer. They develop strength, flexibility and aerobic benefit. However, to do them without a sense of the whole body, the spine, the head-tail connection, is useless in terms of activating a sense of Integration in the whole body. You may be moving your leg, but how are you holding your head? Support the leg by lengthening up through the head and feet. Feel the effect of the movement on your whole spine, organs, arm. Go at your own pace. Move from an inner sense. Be present in the body's experience. You will feel much better when you are finished, with a sense of vibrancy about your whole person, not just a feeling that you have done a chore.

Whatever objects or equipment you use in your exercise routine will influence your experience, body and mind. Machines will promote muscle-building, combatting the forces of gravity directly, grounding in physical presence. Rolling on an exercise ball will promote flexibility and instinctive reflex reactions. Low-to-the-floor trapeze work will promote a combination of strength with mobility, grounding with instinctive flexibility. Think about your needs in your exercise work. Mix different techniques to avoid letting any one routine become so familiar that you do it without attention to the body.

An exercise system can help manage body problems, like problems of alignment. The exercise can provide relief to an area and keep a problem at bay. For example, problems of poor muscle use or over-use can be improved by strengthening muscles around the area which supply additional support. Enough stomach muscle work will keep the lower back from aching even without directly addressing the alignment or usage patterns causing the pain. Nervous tension and habitual body stiffness can be managed with exercise. Exercise reduces stress by dispersing these movement elements, tiring them, leaving the body ready to act as a whole.

"I feel I have more control over my conversation if I have exercised. I don't have to talk out of nervous energy. I feel more grounded."

This predominantly gesture-oriented approach to exercising the body has benefits and dangers. When attending to one area, stress can inadvertently be created in another. Too vigorous an approach to one problem area can increase damage. Keep the whole body under surveillance. Use Integrated Movement when making a transition from one exercise to another. Review critical areas of tension, i.e., the neck and shoulders, for unnecessary strain. Keep a sense of the whole body in supportive alignment for the exercise and let your breath be the integrating aspect.

PROMOTING INTEGRATED MOVEMENT

Exercises using body diagonals involve the whole body and prepare for Integrated Movement. They are not common in most exercise systems but are well developed in the system of movement called Bartenieff Fundamentals^{TM}. These exercises promote an understanding of the diagonal connections from left foot to right arm, activating abdominal obliques and deep spinal muscles. The principle is feeling an active connection of limb and torso, right and left, upper and lower, and front to back of the body.

To experience this, lie on the floor with your arms and legs apart so that the body looks like an "x". Imagine you are stretching large rubber bands diagonally, first through one part of the "x" then through the other. Let the foot rock on the heel and let the momentum carry through one line of the "x." Feel the elasticity through your body. Do not let the shoulder move up and down, but instead, feel that the arm comes out of the middle of your torso. Repeat this on the opposite side.

If you like this experience, you can follow the movement through into a sit-up, exhaling, hollowing the abdomen, feeling the ease with which the body-diagonal brings you to a sitting position. You can fold the x in half, bringing right elbow and left knee together, then alternate, feeling the elasticity of the torso. You can circle one arm over the head making a full circle across the body, feeling the effect throughout the torso and into the legs.

With this preparation, you might experiment with all the body diagonals you can find. Using the momentum created by the first folding and unfolding "x," shift your weight to sitting, to hands and knees, to hands and feet and eventually to standing. Roll, twist, sit up, turn over, feel connected, feel the sense of rubber bands, feel the continuity of movement and a clear beginning and ending.

Playgrounds, especially the swings, provide interesting opportunities to rediscover Integrated Movement.

Start to swing with the usual kick off the ground, until you have a good momentum. Allow the lower body, the swing of the legs, to initiate the movement, while the upper body counterbalances. Feel the moment of extension as you reach out and up with your legs. Feel the contraction as you reverse the movement, legs back, body forward, while folding up. Here the shape of your body is changing contour and dynamics. If you break up this movement into gestures, you are not able to swing high or develop momentum.

In any exercise, as movement travels through the body, there can be spots in which you feel tension or strain, even pain. If you notice this, stop the movement at or near that spot, where the tension is not too extreme.

Focus your breathing into the area of strain. Feel as if a balloon were filling and emptying around that area. Feel each muscle fiber and cell expand and contract. As you inhale, feel you have reached the limits of the cell body wall. The tension, like the sides of the balloon, have increased to their fullest. (The flow is bound.) Now let the air out, feeling the sense of freedom and release. (The flow is free.) Body fluids, lymph, and blood are flowing through the area. Make adjustments until the body can move through the exercise with ease.

INJURY

We usually pay the most attention to the body after an injury. The body's natural defense is to create a 'splint' around the area by tensing the surrounding muscles. This protective instinct increases pain and eliminates Integrated Movement. So, the first step to greater comfort is to reverse this reaction.

Here are some steps you can follow or adapt as a basic approach to reducing the pain of a spasm, sprain, or other injury.

RELIEVING PAIN

Hands On:

1. Put your hands on the area of pain. Breathe.
2. Ask the person you are helping to breathe into the area of pain. The conscious, controlled use of the breath brings movement to the frozen muscles and lets them relax. The attention increases the flow of blood and provides some relief.

Comfort:

3. Make sure the injured person is comfortable and that knees, head, sides of the body are supported. Use pillows.

Support:

4. Go to parts of the body that are far from the injury. If it is in the back, try supporting a lower leg. Move it around. The movement will gently massage muscles near the area of tension. All of this is done slowly with constant attention to the injured person. Fear that a movement will cause pain can cause the person to tense in anticipation. Do very small movements very carefully. Rest. Then try again. Once the movement is familiar, it will not cause pain, but relieve it.

Specific Breath:

5. Ask for specific breath support: "breathe to the count of four, now exhale to the count of four." "Inhale as I lift the leg up. Exhale as I put it down." Give tactile support, and support with your own body weight.
Supporting the weight of the limb with breath and giving careful guidance along the appropriate path often eliminates pain on the second repeat. The body gradually relaxes. The secondary pain leaves. A sense of relief follows. One can now gently massage the area of injury defining and outlining the muscles and bones.

Knee-Drops:

6. If there is upper-back pain, suggest raising both legs in a bent knee position. Let both knees slowly fall to the same side of the body, establishing a diagonal line through the torso. Use very slight

movement and give maximum support. Tremendous release from
pain can be experienced when the diagonal is established in this way.

Arm-Circle:

7. If possible, begin a small circling of the arm away from the injury.
It can start by being confined to the arm socket itself. Gradually
increase the circumference if it seems advisable.
If the pain is in the low back, reverse the sequence of leg and arm
movements.

Natural Breath:

8. As the pain releases, a natural flow of breath returns to the body.
This is the first sign of the return of Integrated Movement.

Changing Position:

9. When the person is ready to change positions, sit or stand, special
attention must be paid to retain the Integrated quality of the movement. Use slow motion. Pause from time to time. Each movement
of a part should be felt throughout the whole body before weight is
taken on the feet. By allowing all body parts to adjust to the areas
taking support, a return of the pain or muscle spasm is avoided.

Be prepared to take your time. You may not do all steps in one session. The
first five steps are enough for a start. Rest, warmth, cold packs and medication
may all be used as well, but movement, attention to breath and the body will
accelerate the recovery process and establish good patterns for the future.

We can learn a great deal from our injuries. For a time after an injury, we
feel the body's needs more acutely. We are more mindful of how we move. We
prepare with the whole body. We feel the movement connections as they travel
through the back and legs. Thus, in a crisis, we take the time to "listen" to the
body. We are open to integrating new information into our daily patterns.

The unspoken goal of much body work is to release blocks to the body's
natural movement and heal the effects of previous injuries. Often, the effects
of physical injury can outlast the actual healing of the injury. Deep body work
can reveal patterns developed around the injury which are still active in the
body.

Sally suffered an ice-skating injury many years ago. While she was healing,
she adopted certain patterns in walking which she later retained. The resulting

imbalance began to cause leg and knee strain. Working with the body, understanding the anatomy and experiencing new ways of moving the foot, she remembered the injury and many painful associations. Now that the old adjustments and the emotions associated with them were acknowledged, new patterns had a better chance of success.

You might wonder how anyone retains any Integrated Movement if it is threatened by every trauma and injury. Integrated Movement is tougher than that. It may be reduced in size, it may have to move around injured or paralyzed parts, but it will be there if there is some vitality and health left in the individual. The blocks are like rocks in a stream. The Integrated Movement flows around them. Special techniques must be used to remove or alter the blocks. The following is one of my favorites.

ENTERING THE BODY CATHEDRAL

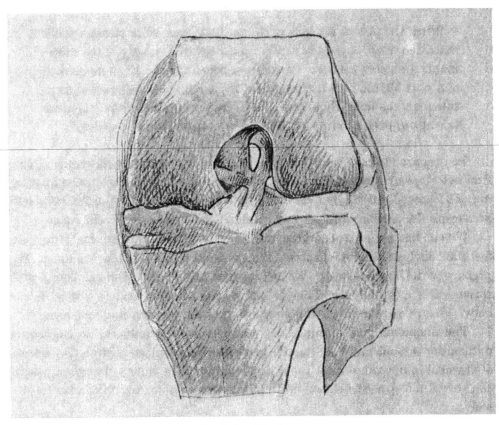

Condyles of the Knee

Shrink like Alice in *Through The Looking Glass* and imagine you are in a giant stone cave shaped like the knee. Study good anatomical photographs of the knee so that you can locate all the bony landmarks. Visualize and experience all the surfaces, curves, protrusions. Become intrigued with the landscape of the knee.

Feel the tunnel through the two condyles (photo) of the femur. Feel the precarious stone roof of the patella, hanging above you. Lounge in the fibers of the meniscus, the cartilage in the knee sockets, as you trace along the cruciate ligaments, which cross diagonally through the knee, rolling and twisting with them, as you did in the "x" roll when you discovered your body diagonal.

Swim in the bursa in the space surrounding the two smooth condyles and sockets of each knee. Feel the sense of the tidal wave as the fluids ebb and flow with the slight movement of flexion and extension. Feel the way the socket-like cup moves to receive the polished curves of the condyles.

Moving very slowly and slightly, picturing the movement as you go, initiate movement at the condyle, ball end. Feel the richness of movement as the whole thigh bone moves and the leg bends, yet feel the receiver of the socket on the tibula end. Enjoy the space between these bones, and the architectural ligaments like steel guide wires defining the limits of movement over a vast space. Brush and lean against these wires, ligaments, encouraging their resiliency. Allow a sense of movement in all three planes, so that you appreciate how spacious a cave you have found.

Also allow the meniscus, which deepens the socket and makes it a very cozy cradle, to initiate movement as it does when you swing the lower leg forward to take a step. Feel how the two bones are partners and reciprocal in movement. The counter rotation will also provide support without a tightening or holding of the muscles.

Movement with this sensitivity is deeply relaxing and engenders relaxation in surrounding muscles. Tears and injuries can heal more quickly before chronic problems set in. Use this technique with any two bones of the body, with organs or between muscle groups. It creates a feeling of space and ease. It relieves the pain of pulls or strains and speeds the return of pain-free movement. It opens a flow of movement to pass through an area, allowing the whole body a sense of connectedness and well-being. The nature of the body itself is such that releasing any one area affects the whole. The body loses the sense of mechanical functioning which is actually most inappropriate for this sensitive, delicate substance.

IMAGE AND METAPHOR

Where do images come from? Why is it that today the rocks around the lake look like a string of pearls around a neck, when they never have before? Images seem to come from a blend of memory, mood and visual experience. Body movement generates images. And the conscious search for the Integrated moment in physical movement intensifies images, thoughts and feelings.

As we become open to this level of consciousness we release a new flow of information to and from the body. We have been studying how our image, conveyed by movement, impacts others in communication. Now we will let the body move and speak directly in its imagistic way. Once you begin listening to the body, it can offer astounding information. I will share Valerie's experience with you so that you can become comfortable letting your own body teach you.

As Valerie moved, she discovered she was not comfortable letting her voice reflect her movement. She felt her voice interfered with a clear expression of Integrated Movement. She felt a tension in her throat when singing or even speaking, which we acknowledged. Her goal was to free the voice to respond to her movement. She lay down on a mat. *"Close your eyes and focus on your breath,"* I said. She noticed that her breath was high in her body, near the throat, not in the abdomen. She experienced an image of a closed gate when the breathe reached her throat. The image arose from her body's experience. A discussion of the gate followed. She looked inside for answers. When she got stuck, I asked her questions. *"What does the gate represent? What is on the other side of the gate? Who has the key?"*

Her voice changed as she described the images. We connected abstract images to her personal life experiences. When she had finished, she began to shift from lying to sitting and then to standing. As she walked around, speaking comfortably, she reported experiencing a new connection between her voice and body.

Spontaneous association is always available beneath the surface of your thoughts. As you try this, you may wish to get the help of a friend or a movement specialist.

> First concentrate on an image. Discover what it means for you.
> Then let your partner ask questions as you speak for the body in
> the first person. The body finds the best image for the moment.
> The body is the teacher and imagery is its language.

THE TEACHER WITHIN

The image your body gives you has meaning beyond the specific movement task. It usually relates to an immediate issue in your life.

In an exercise session using low hanging bars, Ann found she was working with images of strength, of standing tall, taking charge, taking command. As she integrated her movement while climbing the low bars, she felt powerful. *"I was struggling to command space from this position, rather than using my more usual movement patterns of turning and folding. I realized it was exactly the attitude I wanted when meeting very powerful people in my company. Accomplishing the task in a studio with bars and repeating it until there was the ease of Integrated Movements, made it easy to translate to the right frame of mind for the business meeting."*

Using the body as teacher puts the mover in charge of the process, an essential feature for Integrated Movement. The more the mover is in charge, the more she 'owns' the experience. It is absorbed. It is expressed by Integrated Movement. Outside help is often welcome and necessary, but the change is the result of the mover alone.

Imagery and insights come from the movement. In the Western tradition, teachers are active. In the Eastern tradition they are still. The less they do, the more the learner takes responsibility. Then the experience is well-integrated and the student does not become dependent on the teacher to recreate the experience.

Watching yourself on videotape enhances learning since the feedback about the body is immediate:

"I saw how fragmented my movement was. It did not look smooth. I had known this, but after seeing the tape, I was able to create a different inner focus which allowed for a different movement experience. The change was astounding to my teacher as well. Without knowing how, I made the movement integrated and cohesive. Afterwards we talked about what I had changed. I made a shift from focusing on external objects to inner awareness. No one could have told me how to do this."

BLENDING BODY AND VERBAL THERAPY FOR CHANGE

Sadness, depression, exhaustion, are all foes of Integrated Movement. The movement becomes so small it is virtually invisible or breaks up into pieces, gestures and postures. In the extreme, it can even disappear. Times of transition, which usually are stressful, can also show diminished amounts of Integrated Movement as old values are replaced by new ones. Some people can shut out unpleasant things and maintain their full level of functioning. Others become angry, which releases energy and keeps them active and engaged.

Illness produces a lessening of Integrated Movement as we take hot tea and a good book to bed. In long illness, there is a danger of becoming passive, letting others make decisions, even losing interest in our own recovery. All the body's energy is subsumed by the illness. A friend of mine, despite great pain, was able to maintain a sense of well-being. He was dying of cancer yet he stayed fully involved in his life, working to finish things up, until the end. We could talk about his death and there was no apparent change in his Integrated Movement. It was as if he so fully understood what was happening that he treated it as part of his life. He did not express regret. His mental attitude kept him Integrated. It was extremely inspiring.

If a person is disabled, severely handicapped or paralyzed, the parts of the body which remain mobile take over the function of the Integrated Movement. Everything capable of moving will. But when emotional blocks to Integrated Movement occur, they have to be dissolved or at least addressed to allow the regenerative aspects of Integrated Movement to return. How do we do this? One method is psychotherapy.

In verbal therapy the goal is to unearth limiting beliefs and experiences, which block happiness or success. In movement, the goal is to free the body to a range of expression of the dynamics of energy and space. By working with the body, one effects a readiness of mind, which, when it changes, will manifest in the body. Both kinds of therapy seek the goal of harmony of the body-mind state, fulfillment and optimal function. The essence of individuality in movement and the healthy aspects of the personality converge in the moment of Integrated Movement.

E: *"I still find it hard to see how changing the body is going to effect a person's psychological make-up. I see how it can change mood, feelings about things and perceptions, but will perceptions really have an effect on the deep-seated psychological patterns of your personality? Movement work seems irrelevant to understanding past family relationships or issues of self-esteem. In body work, you can avoid issues forever."*

P: *"And you can in verbal therapy too! Some people can work with movement and never make connections to its meaning in their lives. Others can work within their thoughts and never make the changes they want."*

E: *" I saw someone who chose to confine his movement to one small area. He would not extend his body into space. Although there was no physical limitation to traveling, leaping, walking, he remained within a five -foot radius in the room. I asked him to walk around, go to each corner, get a sense of the rhythm and timing of the music and add it to the walk. In time, the inhibition to space was overcome and the experience was quite exhilarating. But there was no automatic application of the awareness to his daily life."*

P: *"One might have to pursue the idea and discuss it with him. As a person becomes aware of movement choices, a sense of participation in events is inevitable."*

E: *"But we have no idea where the limitation came from, how it affects his life, and what it means in his whole personality."*

P: *"But what about all the people in traditional therapy who never seem to change? They might fully understand themselves, but they never seem to change the patterns."*

E: *"But they can. I am reminded of the time Diane, a psychotherapist, worked with a student in a Psychology class. The student spoke about her mother with sadness and tears.*

"We saw Integrated movements at moments of deep concern. We saw the student bring her whole body to bear on the importance of the situation. Then, we saw a larger, clear Integrated Movement when she decided to call her mother and send a Valentine gift.

"We all felt a tremendous sense of relief. The moment of resolution, as seen in the Integrated Movement, may not always happen in the session, but it can still result from the work done there."

P: *"Now suppose someone worked on their body for years and then had some therapy. I think they would change very rapidly. The body would be able to act on new awareness and new perceptions. Movement experience would assist the translation of perception to action."*

THE EVOLUTION OF OUR MOVEMENT

REFLEXES

Reflexes are whole-body instinctive responses which underlie Integrated Movements and insure our basic survival. Reflexes initiate all phases of physical development. Integrated Movement patterns occur as we master each phase of development. They remain with us and evolve as we learn to speak, to take charge of our environment and to interact in our culture.

In the first year of life, the "rooting" reflex initiates head turning movements to look for food and bobbing movements which locate food. Thus, movement in the horizontal plane is established and the ability of the senses to find and identify specific objects develops. (The result is direct and indirect movements, as defined by Laban Movement Analysis.[1]) The first year of life is about discovering the environment.

In its second year of life, the baby pushes and reaches, stands, falls, climbs. The Gallant Reflex, Asymmetrical Tonic Neck reflex and others support the development. The upright pattern of the vertical plane is mastered with a Newtonian-like testing of gravity for the weight of things. (Strength and lightness become total body movements.)

In the infant's third year, forward and backward movements are initiated. Flexion, extension, and lumbar reach is mastered in the sagittal plane, along with a sense of time, accelerating and decelerating.

This is not a linear progression. All the reflex movements are inherent in the infant and are in the process of developing from birth. However, in each of these years, specific movements are mastered as total body actions and became the dominant mode of expression for a time. Each pattern breaks up, disintegrates and reintegrates many times in the course of development as new challenges present themselves.

Such factors as genetics, interplay with the environment, imitation, modeling, education, intellectual and cultural development influence the final selection of style and preference of Integrated Movement. Each pattern of Integrated Movements reflects the history of the individual in some way. Within the range of human movement, there are twelve factorial variations and choices which, in part, allow for our uniqueness of thought and action. This is a basic resource of compelling, integrative, healing, nourishing, expressive movement. Much of what seems like random movement of the baby's arms and legs is actually a freeing and binding of the muscle tension of the body from the spine through the limbs and back. This is called centralizing the flow. It prepares the body for variations in movement dynamics. Centralizing of the body's shape happens with each expansion and contraction of the breath, letting the body grow and shrink.

Centralizing the flow is the first indication of Integrated Movement. Like the amoeba responding to its environment with a total change in shape, so the human baby has this same innate quality to respond to stimuli with a total change of shape or tension. By centralizing the flow of tension and shape through the body, the baby is preparing to take charge of its needs through movement. The limbs and spine are transmitting and receiving consistent qualities of shape and tension through the muscles, bones, organs.

The movement flows from the center of the body outward, then back in, growing and shrinking in response to comfort or discomfort. It differentiates along the axes of the body, from the head to the tip of the spine, side to side and forward to back. As the baby begins to crawl, stand and climb, it is molding space actively, becoming its architect. The baby frees and binds his muscles in response to safety or threat. He releases the tension and deflates to relax. By controlling his muscle tension, he can later direct his hand to exactly what he wants, and brush away what he no longer needs. He can regulate the speed with which he keeps his precious toys away from others, or offers them. His actions express his thoughts, feelings and needs long before he uses language.

When the baby is not totally occupied by his expression, he experiments with extremities, fingers and toes, separating them from the global movement of total expressiveness. Sometimes the play serves self-discovery. Other times, it is an interplay with the parent, testing for beneficial and pleasing effects, mirrored in the parents reactions. The development of gestures and the periphery of the body alternates with the development of the center, the spine.

"The spine is the earliest initiation of the self through space. We are continually reborn with every postural initiation. We are sending ourselves into the universe with each action that travels from mind through body or which may initiate in the body and become transposed through will into action...

"In development, the spine is more active at first and then seems to pass the initiation on to the limbs. The gestures then delineate the periphery, and articulate the environment which it is more developed to do...

"The gesture has more will, the spine has more response. Touch and the hand have one mind; one mind for the extremities, intent. The spine has a different mind; more involved with attention and responsiveness."

" Reach one hand in front of you. Feel your spine respond. Reach a hand in back of you. Feel the moment just before you lose your balance and need to stop. The spine is non-emotional. It is more about being. Hence the stillness of meditation. The gestures are more about doing. The organs are the source of emotion." [2]

THE DEVELOPING BABY

Lie on your stomach, head to one side. Feel like you are just waking up. You are a baby. Feel your mouth brushing against the blanket. Sense the rooting reflex which activates the corners of the mouth to turn towards stimulation. Turn you head slowly to the opposite side, feel it brush the surface you are lying on. In this sleepy state, feel the weight of your head. As you lift it slightly, feel the change in tension along your whole spine.

Put your head down to each side. Feel its weight. Relax. Feel the involvement of the whole body and especially the rotation at the base of the skull. Activate the sense of smell. (Imagine burning wood on a fall day, or the smell of the ocean, or your favorite perfume.) Feel the support this adds from the next lowest vertebrae of the neck. Activate the ears to sound in the same way. Feel the increased involvement of the spine.

Take your time as you do this exercise. Don't move the head until you absolutely must. If you lift it too soon, you will use more superficial muscles, rather than initiating the movement from the senses. Your interest initiates the movement from old brain centers. The stimulation of your senses leads you, activating the smooth muscle support first and the striated muscle groups later.

When you have gone from mouth to ears to nose to eyes and have turned from side to side a few times, pause with your head centered. Let the eyes lead the head further by looking up. Do not squeeze the back of the neck, but let the curve extend as far as possible.

Feel the involvement in the whole cervical spinal curve and the need for support lower along the spine. As you reach up with your eyes to see higher, as if to see someone walking into the room, feel the need to bring in the support of the forearms which are resting alongside your head.

When the adult brings in support of the forearm, it is likely to result in a collapse of the spine, as if only one can work at a time. Instead, feel the greater extension you can achieve when you add the forearms to support the reach of the eyes and head.

If you can, have someone assist you by pushing the top of your head back towards your feet. The compression will let you feel the push through the spine as you fold up onto your heels. (Picture a rabbit hopping. This is a homologous, symmetrical push from the upper to the lower body.) At first the head turning is a gesture, separate from the rest of the spine. As more and more of the senses of the head are used, taste, smell, hearing and sight, more spinal muscles contract to support the head.

Once the spine is strong enough to support itself and the arms have lifted the head far enough from the floor, then the legs can develop their push of the lower spine, until the whole spine can be supported by the limbs, as in crawling. Now, as the arms and spine work together, the hands, fingers and elbows energize different vertebrae and organs along the spine; heart and lungs are activated and respond to these movements. Once the legs develop their push through the toes, ankles, forelegs and thighs, they energize the organs below the diaphragm. Fingers and toes radiate to the pancreas, which integrates upper and lower.

ONTOGENY RECAPITULATES PHYLOGENY

Constant feedback between the limbs and spine integrates developmental patterns. The radiating pattern, seen most clearly in the starfish, encourages us to feel the limbs and head as part of a five-pointed star, connecting at the center, the belly. The baby turning over demonstrates this pattern.

The arms and legs rocking and pushing the spine develop the strength to support the body on hands and knees in a homologous pattern, like frogs. Homolateral movements, like those of the lizard, differentiate right and left half of the body, allowing for climbing. Contralateral patterns cross the body diagonally, like those of dogs and horses, and allow for crawling and later, walking.

Through these movements the spine is strengthening itself for later supporting functions. As each spinal level develops, the organs and glands at that level develop and give support to the spine. Through nerves, muscles and organs, the limbs support the head and spine, first on all fours, then on the feet.

The baby can do more than roll over now. He can push headward and flatten out on his belly, he can push back and fold up on his legs, returning to the original flexed position.

In sitting, the limbs become free to gesture again within the range of the balanced spine. The limbs become supporting when the desire to do something beyond that range mobilizes the child to attempt a larger field of motion. From then on, there is constant alternation between spinal support to allow the limbs to gesture and support of the limbs to allow mobility of the spine. To some degree, both are always supporting and active.

Now that you appreciate the stages of the baby's development, let's relate actively to a few examples of the animal movements they mirror.

THE STARFISH AND THE BABY

Starfish:

Curl up into a little ball. Extend your limbs slowly, pretending you are a starfish. Your arms and legs come from the center of your body. Find all the ways you can open and close yourself. Feel that the movement doesn't skip any spots, but flows consistently from the center to the periphery of your body, pauses, then flows back again.

Your stomach, in the middle of your body, is now your mouth. You take in nourishment through your middle, and digest it. Let your head-tail orientation change. You are now centered around your middle.

Let your spine become another limb. Move by means of all five appendages. You are now experiencing navel radiation, similar to the baby in utero, nourished through the belly-button.

Feel the Integrated Moment as the whole body extends or contracts. The movement starts small, in the center of your body. It continues until every part is involved.

Now, imagine each cell is a little starfish. Nourishment seeps in through the body wall, and goes to the nucleus. Each cell in its fluid is like the starfish in water. Each cell pulses and shimmers. Use this sensation to heal or nourish any area of the body.

The centrally radiating movement of the starfish is a large part of the baby's movement experience.

Lie on your back for a moment and wave your arms and legs about, stirring up the air. Feel the arms and legs reaching from the supporting belly, keeping senses of the head active; listen, smell, taste.

Now roll onto your stomach and do the same thing. Feel how strong the stomach has to be to keep all five appendages in the air at the same time.

Notice how active your spine is; how the organs support the limbs; how involved the pelvic, abdominal, thoracic, skull organs are; feel the flow centralizing and dispersing through the body, pulling in, then releasing out.

How limiting are these movements? What are the limits of your world?

The Caterpillar and Spinal Movement:

The caterpillar is an excellent example of total spinal movement. It can feel and reach with its antennae and pull all of its segments up to go forward. It can initiate movement backwards equally well. It can reach and pull and hold with its tail. But, the caterpillar can't jump.

Make yourself a caterpillar. Let your arms and legs become part of your torso. Use the segments of your spine as a caterpillar would. Use your arms to feel the next leaf and to explore the grass.

In this exercise, your spine is your main means of locomotion. You are oriented by head and tail, rather than five arms around a middle. How does it compare?

Undulating spinal movements, characteristic of worms and fish, strengthen our awareness of spinal participation in Integrated Movement. An active spine supports the limbs to reach out into space. Active limbs, as in the star fish, strengthen the spine.

The Rabbit and Homologous Movement:

> Lie on your stomach and pull your upper body back towards your legs, tucking your toes against the floor so that you shift your weight onto your feet like a rabbit.
>
> Push off both legs and catch yourself with your hands, both at once. Feel the push of the legs and the reach of the arms, the airborne moment. Enjoy the extension, the lightness, the forward momentum.
>
> Let the activeness of the belly and organs energize the movement. Do not just let them be carried along. Reverse the hop, starting from the hands first. Push back from your arms. Reach with the legs and tail. Send the energy through the tail end of your spine. Direct the senses of the head back through the tail and legs.

Commit yourself fully to each movement. They draw on impulses and reflexes once very strong, but displaced by other large movement patterns. Feel how these patterns strengthen your current patterns of walking, running, mountain climbing, swimming, etc.

Let your body take charge. After you have gotten the idea, don't plan the movement. Surprise yourself with how fast you can go, how you can trust the space behind you as you go backwards. Enjoy the strength of the pattern and the way your body instinctively seems to know about it. The reflexes underlying these patterns are the foundation of Integrated Movement.

THE HEAD-TO-TAIL CONNECTION

An awareness of spinal movement is essential to an awareness of Integrated Movement. Once spinal action is complete, limb action begins. Proximal sections develop first. The scapula becomes the wings, extending the movement of the spine into space and supporting it. The pelvis, legs and feet allow the spine freedom to travel the earth and leap off of it, briefly.

Imagine that the spinal cord is a tadpole and the brain is the top of it. Feel the smooth, liquid feeling through your spinal chord, the strong layers of muscles on the outside and the fluid running inside. Feel that you are following the fluid as it flows towards the head, then towards the "tail." Allow this to release the long muscles along the spine and the deep small ones between each vertebrae.

> Fold up like a cat at rest, legs tucked under you, forehead touching the floor. Keep your hands close to your ears and your elbows alongside your head.
>
> Lift your weight from your forelegs onto your head, slowly, regulating the weight on your head with your arms. Let your weight roll to the top of your head, rounding your spine as you go.
>
> Roll back and forth, experiencing all the vertebrae of the spine, including the neck. Feel the transfer of weight through the spine and skull. Let the skull be part of the spine.
>
> Open your mouth as you begin to push the head back, making a very small movement. Close your mouth, bringing the upper jaw to the lower to bring your head back. This allows you to feel a release at the base of the skull.

As you open and close your mouth, notice how this activates the spine. We are used to moving the lower jaw in talking and eating. But when we move the upper jaw, we are moving the skull. This distinguishes the skull from the first vertebrae and frees movement to flow easily through the neck vertebrae. By means of this movement, the whole digestive system is reminded of its support for the spine.

Your Upright Spine:

How does your upright posture feel to you now?

> Now tuck your toes under your body when the weight is forward and as it returns, let your weight transfer to your feet.
>
> At the moment of suspension, draw your hands in close to the body, flexed, like a chipmunk's, and come to a standing position, with your knees bent.
>
> Reach up with your head, letting your arms bounce out and then down, as you regain a fully upright position.
>
> Repeat this movement so that you feel your spine is as active as it was when you placed your head on the floor.

Sensations Of Spinal Movement:

- ❖ Have someone tickle you with a feather.
- ❖ Get "the shivers" over a scary thought.
- ❖ Withdraw into yourself, feeling mistrustful or wary.
- ❖ Push something away with your head, like a soccer ball.
- ❖ Wiggle into a wet bathing suit.
- ❖ Walk around balancing something on your head.

Spinal movement activates the central core of the body, the spinal cord and the organs. This is the "center," referred to in meditation and dance. It is both anatomical and metaphoric. As such, both approaches are helpful when you want to connect to deep movement sources or center your mind.

RESPONSES TO SPINAL WORK

"As I work with the simple movement of rolling from head to tail, I relax more and more. I begin to feel that I am shutting out the environment. My inner sensation is as if my organs are moving me. I can feel differentiated masses: brain, lungs, intestines. It's as though I can see inside. I become focused on the movement itself.

"I visualize the shape, function and texture of the anatomy. I am within my own shell and that shell is the end of my world."

"The thought is inside the body, and there is no distinction between mind and body."

"The head-tail exercise made me feel more solid. It awakened a deep center, a source of energy. My voice sounded lower. Since the exercise is a bridge between the lowest energy of the spine and the highest in the head, it is a whole journey. I felt a kind of primitive wisdom. I also got in touch with releasing the front of my body. This took me away from the feeling of 'exercise' and into awareness of my own being. I felt refreshed. It gave me a momentary vacation."

DEVELOPMENTAL PATTERNS AND THE ORGANS

Each part of the body has a direct relationship with an organ: the kidney relates to the knees, the ankles to the reproductive organs. Less familiar in the West, these connections are known in Eastern body systems, like Shiatsu and Yoga. Bonnie Cohen, Founder and Director of the School for Body/Mind Centering, is developing methods for using this information to heal disabilities in children and for active body training.

> Rest your hand on your knees, but keep your elbows free to move. Breathe slowly and deeply. As your ribs move, feel your scapula move, then your whole upper arm. The lungs are actually moving your arms.

We can analyze the body through muscle and skeletal work, which is familiar to most people. We can also think about the body in terms of specific organs or body systems, the digestive system, fluids and nerves.

The organs of the body form the mesentery. They are continuous with the outer body. The contents and the container are one, and move each other. Therefore it is logical that we should be able to contact the organs, the inner level, from the outer limbs and vice versa.

"The viscera are ever-changing both their shapes and their positions. They move with the movements of the diaphragm and of the interior abdominal wall." (*Grant's Method of Anatomy*, J.V. Basmajian, MD, p.202.) Organs move all the time: by breathing, by their weight and function. Just as breathing is partly voluntary and partly involuntary, we can permit a more autonomous movement, or we can apply our consciousness and move them at will. *"[Organs] move when the posture alters, being highest (in the body) when the subject is recumbent, lower when he sits, and lowest when standing. The hollow organs, stomach, intestines, bladder, uterus vary as they fill and empty. Fear and other emotions result in relaxation of the stomach so that the greater curvature suddenly falls."*

We have all experienced "a sinking feeling" in the pit of the stomach or the heart-racing thrill of excitement. We are used to thinking our organs are out of our conscious control. If they are, it is because we have never tried to put them into our awareness. (See Bonnie Cohen material.) Putting internal organs into our awareness is very different from a doctor's view and knowledge of organs. We are listening to our bodies for inspiration, self-knowledge and self-healing.

PRINCIPLES FOR MOVING INTERNAL ORGANS

When you want to experience the movement of an internal part, look at photographs of it. Locate the specific organ in your body. Trace its shape. Use your hands to find it on your body, or move the organ as if it is in your hands. Simultaneously, feel the movement inside your body. Once it "wakes up," let the organ dictate the movement. It will probably involve a whole body shape change or energy change. Relax and enjoy a feeling of automatic movement. When you are able to tap the power of the organs, you may find you are able to do difficult things more easily.

Take your right hand and put it on your right kidney, alongside your spine between your right iliac crest (rim of the hip), and your lowest rib. Look at pictures of the kidney, and transfer that knowledge to your body. The size of your hand is just about right, although the kidney is a bit smaller. As your hand conforms to your back, it makes just the kidney-shaped curve.

Do the same with your other hand. Give the kidneys a little massage. Close your eyes and picture them. Make contact. Now, arch and round your back a little. Feel you are doing this from the bones, the spine. Your hands, acting for the kidneys, are being moved, being pushed and squeezed a little. You feel a change in your hand, perhaps your wrist flexed. Keep it a small movement, just around the area of the kidney.

Stop. Have your hands tell your kidneys to go forward, and let your spine react. Let the hands, acting for the kidneys, give them a little push to start. "My hands send a message to the kidneys to go forward and come back." Once contact is made to the organ, it will direct you.

As the movement starts, you may wish to release your hands. Use them as helpers periodically. Feel you can now widen the kidneys away from each other, leading with the bottom or the top. Let them scroll forward and back. Feel them alternate, one forward, one back.

Now that you know the feeling in your own body, try feeling the movement on someone else. Notice the change when your friend experiences the shift of initiation from the supporting structures to the organ.

You are now experiencing your body differently. Your second experience will be easier, as you are in a new body-level awareness.

The Brain:

Move your hand over your skull. This is the container. Go "inside." What do you find? The brain. Sense the parts of the brain. Draw a line over your eyebrows, and around the top of your ears, down to the hairline. This is the size of your brain.

Then differentiate the forebrain, the two halves of the cerebellum, midbrain and medulla. The medulla connects to the spinal cord, so you have to go down through the pons to the spinal cord. The spinal cord is part of the brain.

Sense the brain extending down through the spinal cord, to its end, at the last thoracic vertebrae, then as it fans out into a very dense nerve system.

E: *"At first I was sitting, looking and listening. My consciousness was in front of my eyes. Maybe it's just my imagination, but when I began the exercise, I felt a sense of energy going to the back of the skull. I felt a change from being on the surface, to an inner awareness."*

S: *"All of a sudden, my face was not just a surface, but was part of a volume with depth."*

R: *"I felt like I was under a low hat, with a brim. That was the skull."*

D: *"I felt like Cro-Magnon Man. The brain felt heavy. I felt a sense of the weight of the organ, the density, the position, the activity, the strain."*

Rub between your eyebrows. The pituitary is right there under the front of the brain which balances on the pituitary gland. It is pea-shaped, and directs the hormones of the whole body. When you absent-mindedly rub your forehead, you may be seeking stimulation of this gland.

The Adrenals:

> Feel the gland, location, size and shape. Feel the center. Pump it up with air, like filling a bicycle tire. Make a hissing sound as you pump the air in short spurts, sensing the organ fill. Once full, let the air all out with one long hissing sound.

Jane felt her adrenals were stuck in a state of panic. First, we 'pumped' air into them. We then felt the balance of the two adrenals and compared them. We gently sensed movement of the organs in the sagittal (wheel) plane, the vertical (door) plane and the horizontal (table) plane, experiencing the borders and surfaces. Jane shaped her hands to correspond with the adrenals, letting them move with the support and counter-tension of the kidneys underneath it.

The hand movements were slow and sensitive, calming the adrenal and allowing a more resilient sense of the lower body. As Jane sensed the adrenal gland resting lightly on the kidney, this became the impetus for a movement exploration which involved the whole body in support of the adrenals. The arms and legs moved gently, in a delicate dance. Gradually the fingertips and toes participated. Her face expressed the sadness which before had been locked in the gland and hidden from awareness.

The spine is unemotional. Organs are emotional. (Used in this way, "emotional" does not mean happy or sad. It means invested with feeling.) Emotional investment, with organ involvement, is evident in Integrated Movement. If you are working with the bones, you might miss organ stress. Sometimes the organs are responsible for lack of motivation. The skeleton might move, but it seems hollow. If you can find and energize the right organ, or release a tension that is holding it, the motivation returns.

Question: *"Is this the way it should feel? As I was speaking and doing this exercise, my movement slowed down. I sensed I was just below the diaphragm, like being under water, under the middle consciousness. I felt a relaxation throughout my body as the organ initiation took over. My shoulders and face muscles relaxed."*

Answer: *"Yes. That is the kind of experience many people seem to have."*

Question: *"Do you mean that if I want to move my kidneys to the left I can do it?"*

Answer: *"Yes, I do. Your kidneys are moving all the time, why should you not have the ability to move them? Once you start to work with it, gradually you will trust the experience."*

Question: *"How do I know when my body movement is originating from an organ?"*

Answer: *"Put your hand behind your back. Move it. From where I stand, I don't know if you are moving your hand or not. But you know." (Response by Bonnie Bainbridge Cohen in LIMS workshop.)*

Question: *"I am trying to understand it logically. I don't think there are muscle attachments to the organs. So when you are talking about organs moving, are you talking about the surroundings and the breath as the source of initiation?"*

Answer: *"It seems so at first. A feeling of inactivity precedes the experience. Muscling through an old pattern feels active, this does not. The function and activity of the specific organs generate the movement, rather than muscle attachments. You consciously contact the function and the life of the organ as it moves. We are asking it to create a support for the container out of which it was formed. Keep your doubt and your mistrust. Your questions will lead to your most important discoveries and answers."*

WISDOM OF THE CHAKRAS

Bringing your consciousness to the Chakras may help you perceive your own involvement in Integrated Movement. The Chakra energy centers lie along the spine and correspond to endocrine glands and are supported by developmental patterns. The postures of Yoga serve to open each center, allowing movement to be activated easily along the spine. Each organ needs to be self-supporting and each Chakra needs to participate in the whole.

The seven Chakras are metaphors, abstract places in the body. You can visualize the seven Chakras as seven glands. This allows a person access to a range of expression from the instinctual sexual level, including self-love and hate, to the most evolved level, that of enlightenment and contact with one's spiritual essence. The Root Chakra is the first, corresponding to the coccygeal body. The seventh and final is the Crown Chakra, corresponding to the pineal gland.   All centers rely on each other, just as the developmental patterns rely on support from the preceding one. If the lower patterns are weak, all the later ones reflect that. You arrive at the next level when one phase of development is fulfilled. The preceding pattern has to propel you into the next one.

Strengthening the Chakra center from which the pattern originates releases the emotions stored in that center.

Strengthen a center by:

❖   Using the appropriate Yoga postures;

❖   Breathing into the related gland or organ;

❖   Finding the movements and sounds which come from or go to that center.

The following exploration of the relationship of the Chakras to movement is based on conversations with Pamela Ramsden, drawing on her experience of the Chakras, and my understanding of Bonnie Bainbridge Cohen's theories.[3] It is a rudimentary exploration intended to stimulate your own discoveries. Let your own body's wisdom guide you.

THE ROOT CHAKRA

The root Chakra refers to grounding, contact with the planet, having a purpose. You are here for a purpose, you are centered and grounded in that purpose. It is located at the base of the spine or coccyx. It feels like touching a warm stone. It is an anchor which goes to the center of the earth. This corresponds to the coccygeal body and the developmental pattern of a homolateral yield and push from the lower limbs. Folding up into the flexed baby position puts you in touch with this center.

THE BELLY (SACRAL) CHAKRA

The location is below the navel and it corresponds to the gonads. The focus is relationships. Creative energy springs from this center, as well as feelings of aggression or passivity.   Your feelings well up, like a wave or a volcano, expressed as outrage or jealousy. The angry side could be like molten lava and the calm side, like contentment, lying in the warm sun. It is sensual and sexual too. Anger or a tantrum would be one way to get in touch with this center. The developmental pattern for this Chakra is the homolateral yield and push from the upper limbs.

THE SOLAR PLEXUS CHAKRA

The solar plexus is located between the navel and the top of the sternum. The solar plexus is the meeting of animal and spiritual. It seems to correspond to the adrenals and pancreas, which is like the horizon in the body that separates upper and lower. If it is blocked, you have trouble getting from one state to the other. You are either being a saint or a horrible, loathsome creature. You also have trouble being like your contented, purring cat.

There is a close affinity between Integrated Movement and this Chakra because the moment of integration has the same quality of passing from one state to another, of joining the upper and lower body. Here the developmental pattern is the homologous yield and push from the lower limbs.

HEART CHAKRA

We feel a sense of longing from this center. It's the feeling of loving someone so much "it hurts." The positive side to this is compassion; going to the movies and crying with joy; looking at your child; wanting to help a starving beggar.

When this center is closed, you find ways not to feel the pain. When stuck in this center, you feel you could drown in a sea of tears. If the heart Chakra is balanced, you can feel compassion but you don't drown in it and therefore you can be more effective.

Gland-like structures just under the heart, called 'heart bodies' are the anatomical relationship to this center. The movement is a homologous reach and push from the upper limbs. (Picture the baby pushing on its arms to lift its head.) The chest lifts to the bottom of the sternum. You can also stimulate this center from the thymus gland with a homologous reach and pull from the upper limbs.

THROAT CHAKRA

The throat Chakra has to do with articulating and expressing yourself. In words, art, music, or whatever form you choose, it is also the art of listening.

When this center is stuck, the expression of feelings gets stuck. When its open, its like an outpouring. Picture a flock of birds taking off. Rapid vibrations of the tongue, fluttering sounds of Yemenite Jews and Native American Indians capture this quality. The body has to be very grounded to allow this full expression.

The corresponding glands are the thyroid and parathyroid. The developmental pattern relating to the thyroid is the homologous reach and pull of the lower limbs, the body moving backwards, as in the backward rabbit hop, pushing off the arms, reaching with the tail.

The pattern relating to the parathyroid is the contralateral reach and pull with the upper and lower limbs, a complex pattern, needing full participation of the earlier patterns. (Add also the carotid bodies with a spinal yield and push from the tail.)

Some people let the flood-like outpouring happen from the throat Chakra. If it takes over, everything else shuts down. The communication gets lost. All you can relate to is the imbalance.

"Our strengths are our weaknesses," said Bonnie, one day. We never get stuck in our weak area, but we can overuse our strengths and not know how to stop. All centers don't have to be equal. We just have to be able to 'change our mind,' to have a momentary shift of center, a new perspective and get the appropriate support. The strength becomes tired and needs it's shadow, its complement, to renew it.

THE THIRD EYE

The Chakra of the third eye and the pituitary gland, lie between the eyes. The experience of it is like a dance, the dance of fantasy and vision. It is precognition: knowing something before it happens, seeing things others don't see. It knows things, not rationally, it just "knows." You could call it the "inner bell."

The third eye has an energy vibration like a gyroscope or flashing lights or shooting stars. Without it there is no sense of psychic discovery, no intuition, no fun. The fun and silliness come from the pituitary. You can do lots of work from this center. The pituitary is the overseeing gland. It relates to seeing and the developmental pattern of a spinal reach and pull from the tail. A spinal reach and pull from the head will activate the mammillary bodies which also enhance this Chakra.

THE CROWN CHAKRA

This is the pineal gland which perceives light. It was actually a precursor of the eye. In some animals, it still functions as the eye. The developmental pattern is a spinal yield and push from the head. This center radiates light, connects to the center of the universe, wholeness, or the cosmos. If it were a sound, it would be sustained and harmonious. Picture a calm ocean, a horizon.

You gain a tolerance for other people from this center. It's an acceptance we experience when we watch people's Integrated Movement. Perhaps we let go of our judgmental state when we experience the Crown Chakra.

If you are operating from this center downwards, the pineal gland radiates towards the core of your being. You are infusing spirit into your body. You need to be welling up from the root which brings you strength and gives form to your spirit.

When the body is fully rounded, head to knees as in the head-tail exercise or the plow position of yoga, the cycle completes by a leap of energy from root to crown, or coccygeal body to pineal. Picture the crescent moon and complete the cycle from one tip to the other.

If all the Chakras were perfectly open, would the movement be perfectly Integrated? I wonder.

Life-size bronze sculpture titled, "The Right Light"

TEN

THE ART OF LIFE

A work of art is like a prolonged Integrated Movement. In many applications throughout previous chapters, we have used Integrated Movement to address issues of thought and movement in relation to expression. Now I would like to expand the use of Integrated Movement to the arts. To me, this is a natural step because Integrated Movement implies changing perception, being in touch with oneself, one's expressiveness, and perceiving differently. These are all qualities we need to bring to an appreciation of art, and which art asks of us.

The magic and the message of a work of art can become accessible when we look for the integrative quality in it, just as it does when we look for a person's Integrated Movement in communication.

Many of us feel insecure when we approach a work of art and do not know how to respond to it. Through posture, gesture and Integrated Movement, though, we can all perceive the message and impact of a work of art.

We can ask ourselves:

❖ What is the consistent theme in this piece?

❖ What is repeated?

❖ Around what forms does everything organize?

❖ What consistent feeling do I get from this?

Just the process of doing this itself feels integrative, helps to clarify the artist's statement, and makes our own deep response to the work accessible. We engage more fully in the work and gain more from it.

Art is also a mirror. Like movement it shows us what we need to know about ourselves. Art exists in the cracks and crevices of life, in the in-between places that usually go unnoticed. The sculptor George Segal uses posture to ask us to face ourselves as we really are. (The figures are so life-like you have to touch them to see if they are breathing.) In his piece *Three People On Four Park*

Benches, at the Pepsico sculpture garden in Purchase, New York, the artist invites us to study the postures of a group of ordinary people. We remember someone we know now who sits slouched on a park bench, looking lonely and dejected. Or, perhaps what we see is a projection of ourselves as we might one day be. Because it is art, we study it intently, instead of politely averting our eyes.

Life-size bronze sculpture titled, "Taxi"

J. Seward Johnson Jr.'s figure of a man hailing a taxi cab on New York's Park Avenue and 48th Street captures an Integrated Movement reflecting our furious race against time. He confronts us directly with ourselves. His work is explicitly captures the essence of postures, gestures and Integrated Movements, that I have used examples throughout this book.

Another way an artist highlights the mundane elements of life is the use of scale. If an object is huge, larger than life, then surely for a moment we will stop taking that item for granted.

Claes Oldenburg, Installation at the Green Gallery, 1962

"I am for an Art that is political-erotical-mystical, that does something other than sit on its ass in a museum.

I am for an Art that grows up not knowing it is art at all. An Art given a chance of having a starting point of zero.

I am for an Art that involves itself with the everyday crap but still comes out on top.

I am for an Art that imitates the human, that is comic, if necessary, or violent, or whatever is necessary.

I am for an art that takes its mark from the lines of life and twists and extends and accumulates and spits and drips, and is heavy and coarse and blunt and sweet and stupid as life itself." From Claes Oldenburg's Store Days, (Something Else Press, 1967), p. 39.

This view of art is not about imitating something pretty in nature or even about expressing emotions. Oldenburg has taken our implements and made us aware that these are our totems. Andy Warhol has shown us our gods and goddesses, the images we worship. These artists, and others, show us ourselves, our attitudes and values, much as we would look at the relics of an ancient culture.

POSTURE, GESTURE AND INTEGRATED MOVEMENT IN ART

THE WARM-UP

One day, two movement experts walked through New York City's Metropolitan Museum of Art. Their mission: to identify Integrated Movement in art. It was an expedition worthy of great explorers. But this team consisted of myself and Pamela Ramsden, armed with two tape recorders and sturdy walking sneakers. You can do the same. (You don't need the tape recorder, but a good companion is a must!)

Finding the postures and gestures was our warm-up. We entered the area of the museum devoted to 2456 BC Egypt. In the royal family grouping, we noticed that the women were small, the wife and daughter reached only the height of the King's knees. In another sculpture from this period, the King had his arm around his wife, whose head reached to his shoulder. His hand rested on her bosom. The male figures seemed to depict stability, authority and power, by postures and gestures that infer a male dominance. The men all had clenched fists. The women stood straight, showing no particular gesture, depicted as being in "a woman's place," i.e., subordinate.

THE GATEWAY

We entered the gateway to the Maori exhibit, under the inscription: "Where there is artistic excellence there is human dignity."

PR: *"How can we say that something so obviously still, as a sculpture, reflects Integrated Movement?"*

EG: *"Well, if everything in the sculpture is consistent with one movement quality, then I feel we can call it Integrated. In this piece, there is an emphasis on lengthening in an upward direction, a total feeling of lift in every part of the sculpture. It lifts me as look at it. I feel a lifting movement in my spine. Even if it isn't actually moving, the quality of lengthening is consistent in all the gestures and becomes an integrating concept. Do you sense the Integrated Movement in the feet, as they lengthen?*

The piece does not have to look like a person doing an Integrated Movement, although looking at a sculpture of the human form is a good way to begin searching for it. Integrated Movement is equivalent to a consistent movement theme. An abstract element, a curve, or shape, a quality of movement can embody the concept and carry through the piece."

PR: *"Now I see. The posture is the line through the spine, which is an upward, backward curve. The gestures are the four spokes rising out of it, which repeat the curve. There is no contradiction between posture and gesture here and no contradiction in what is represented. A war god and chief also represents peace and superiority."*

Our method:

❖ Start by identifying the gesture(s); then the quality of the gesture.

❖ Next, observe whether it is consistent in all the elements of the piece.

❖ Finally, identify a mood or association to the piece as a result of the movement elements.

One sculpture we studied seemed to have only gestures. They were like intricate designs. Its message seemed to remain tightly woven within the work. We needed to move closer to study it. Yet in another piece, a strong total Integrated Movement quality seemed to reach out to us.

THE HUMAN FORM IN PRIMITIVE ART

The human form, including distortions and enlargements, is often used in primitive art to represent concepts. By relating our own bodies to a work of art, we have a common point of reference. We can use everything we have learned about posture, gesture and Integrated Movement and the way we transmit meaning in our every day movement to understand the thoughts and feelings inherent in works of art.

The body was the dominant presence throughout the Maori exhibit. Male legs formed the gateway and entrance to the exhibit. We entered through a male pelvis. Thus, we were "born" into the male domain. He protected the house and represented his ancestors. Other pieces showed figures with bulging bellies and rounded legs, so we looked for bulging as a theme. The knees bulged, the stomach, the little children's bodies bulged under the big papa figure. Bulging itself signifies pleasure: a full belly, food, a baby. The forehead bulged, as did the nose and mouth. These shapes give us a pleasurable feeling of growing and fullness. A "growing" movement shows satisfaction and pleasure, as in comfort.[3] Reflect on your own feeling of comfort and how you express it in a growing movement as well; a smile of satisfaction rather than a frown.

The more we studied the objects, the more obvious the pattern of growing became. The theme was too consistent to be accidental. At least in part, the purpose of this work must have been to present a feeling of well-being. We were pleased to realize this and felt a shared communication with the culture.

THE PROCESS

We experienced the concept by putting ourselves in the movement, then translated our feeling into words. To experience Integrated Movement in sculpture, follow these steps:

❖ Imitate the piece with your body. Image you are that sculpture. *"The body and shoulders are distorted, accentuating the face. The face is almost as big as the body. I am this large figure, with two small ones across my chest."*

❖ Describe the feeling to yourself or a friend: *"I feel I am bigger than life, and able to protect others, all of whom are smaller."*

❖ Let the interpretation strike you: *"The figure seemed godlike or supernatural. It had a power or force about it that was superhuman. The smaller figures seemed to be on a more human scale. We read the inscription; a chief, a god, with his wife and two children. The description confirmed our observations."*

Looking at the arts sensitively heightened our perceptions to our surroundings. As we left the museum, a jumble of junk on the street became an arresting pattern. Later in the day, I heard the familiar sound of crickets. I thought of electronic music and noticed how the crickets were conducted to a precise ending. My friend was sitting on the sofa, but momentarily, I framed her into a timeless portrait, as if she were in a painting. These were special moments.

MOVING INTO A PAINTING

> First, walk towards and away from a painting. See how your movement, in relation to the painting, changes the way you see it. Does the painting change as you walk? Feel the point when you are at the spot the artist was when she painted it; where you walk "into" the painting. (Do not be daunted if it is an aerial view.)
>
> What are the pathways of your focus? What parts call for your attention? Where was the artist's focus? Why has she chosen this? What is she saying by making this choice?
>
> What seems to unify this scene? What is the artist's mood? What is yours? The Integrated Movement principle will become evident through these questions.

Seen in this way, the painting becomes a bridge, connecting the painter, looking at his subject, and we the viewer, looking at the painting. The painting is a time machine. The work of art can transcend time, culture, society, location. It can show us what existed once in a way that gives us an immediate experience. This is quite miraculous for a culture accustomed to instant world-wide communication. Technology has advanced communication across space, but not across time, and usually without the richness and subtlety of artistic expression.

By placing yourself within the painting, by moving around it and feeling your way into its environment, you will discover a principle that unifies it. This concept will unravel more of the painting than you might have otherwise seen. The postures can be thought of as the structural elements of the composition: the tall trees, a cluster of rocks, or a dense area of color, critically positioned. The posture may also be the relationship of positive and negative space, or the outlines of figures. The gestures may be the themes, objects, symbols, brush stroke or highlights of color. The use of each element will determine whether it functions as a posture, gesture or a part of the main theme. No rules can be made. Each element can be used differently by different artists. You will have to evaluate each one as you see it.

INTEGRATED MOVEMENT IN PAINTING

My observation began as I approached the painting, *Rocks (With Oak Tree)* by Vincent van Gogh. I moved forward and backward and side to side in front of it for a while and became aware of the detail of the background and foreground. It seemed as if it had been painted from two places at once. The rocks in the foreground and the trees in the background were equally detailed. As a viewer, I felt suspended between these two forces, locked into the landscape. This feeling of tension made me aware of every detail. The play of the distance between the two became, for me, the key to experiencing the power and force of the painting.

I stopped thinking about the literal information in the painting, the reputation of the artist, or historical facts. I saw it for myself. That is the goal: to find any integrative principle which lets you experience a painting deeply.

Use the photograph, Vincent van Gogh's *Wheat and Cypress Trees* and follow the questions on the opposite page to experience Integrated Movement in painting for yourself.

Move your head side to side while looking at the photograph of the cypress tree. Move between the tree on the right and the two bushes on the left.

Turn to follow the direction of the bushes towards the left.

Twist and pull slightly backward to the left.

Untwist and go forward, right and upward to the tip of the tree on the right. This upward diagonal pull organizes the form of the painting. The line of rocks tumble between them.

Continue to twist in your body. Get smaller and bigger.

Walk around the landscape with that feeling. Is there anywhere you can't go?

Do you feel more rushed and quicker in the left half of the painting and more serene as you approach the cypress?

What happens when you get to the top of the tree?

How do the light clouds effect you as they drop behind the rocks?

What pulls the painting together most for you, the twisting or the diagonal line?

Where does your eye go most often? Mine goes to the clump of bushes. These are little racing gestures which keep the movement very alive for me. They have a different pulse from the billowing curves of the sky.

QUALITIES OF MOVEMENT

Narrowness:

Les Alicamps by Vincent van Gogh

> Look at the street scene and feel the boundary created by the row of trees.
>
> Narrow into the spaces between the tree trunks. Feel how they compress in the distance.
>
> Feel the narrowness of the tree trunk itself. Cross to the other side of the path. Feel the row of trees creating that border.
>
> Enter the path at the lower left of the picture which seems to be the position of the painter. Feel the sustaining pull into the upper right hand corner as the paths converge. Do you feel the sides of your body narrowing?
>
> Does this give you a sense of tallness, like the verticality of the trees?

As I studied this painting, I felt like an outsider. The trees kept reminding me of bars. But why? Then, as I was describing the movement of narrowness, I realized I was outside of the bars. I was as if imprisoned in my loneliness in contrast to the couple and their companionship. They were together, I alone. I did not seek an interpretation. The description of movement in the painting unleashed it in me.

What is your reaction?

Spikiness; Strength; Quickness:

Pollard Willows with Setting Sun by Vincent van Gogh

> The gnarled tree trunks are like the large bones of your body, the femur, perhaps.
>
> Feel the power of your leg muscles as if they were working into the ground along this shape.
>
> Now rush along your skin with the rhythm of the grass.
>
> Feel the poking thrust of the grass, the branches and the sun's rays, in every layer of the painting.
>
> Feel the spikes thrust through the space as the sun's rays mute and soften the background energy, enveloping the grove, keeping the energy from disappearing into the horizon and bringing it back to you, the viewer.

Note your reactions:

Directness:

Somonsire (Self-portrait) by Vincent van Gogh

The artist's eyes are focused on himself at the center of the painting, unswerving. To penetrate his focus, my own focus intensified. I stared back, looking into the artist's eyes, seeing him as he saw himself. A green luminescence vibrates and swirls around his head. The color and shape make the head seem sculpted out of the painting. Each stroke directs the feeling which streams out at us. I was pulled into the intenseness of the artist's focus. Nothing competed with it. There were no distracting gestures.

Note your reactions:

Shape:

Arcarea, or *Les Joyeusettes* by Paul Gauguin

Shape and color can overlap in a way that outlines the form through the painting. The viewer can travel the edges between color and move along surfaces as if the work were three-dimensional. A continuous mass is created by the forms. This was the integrating theme for me.

THE CONCEPT EMERGES

Art encourages a shift of perception like the one we have to make to see Integrated Movement. In the twentieth century, art also experienced a shift, probably influenced by tribal art. It suggested new artistic options, double meanings, overlapping symbols, and illusions.

Picasso's famous handle bars and bicycle seat becomes a bull. The bull appears, then the bicycle parts. Our minds conceptualize the bull in spite of the obvious nature of the material used. "Conception overrides perception," wrote Picasso himself, to his friend Solomon.[7] Perception itself was now a subject in art and we are expected to be engaged on many levels.

In Max Ernst's *Interior of Sight*, the form of the stone suggests the bird. The eye of the bird becomes the egg. The movement quality of the work is circular and direct, overlapping and continuous. In a Kwele mask, the eyes are placed along a vertical axis, suggesting a nose. The shape is at once an eye, the spine, a tree trunk, an open nut with a seed inside.

The effect of art as ritual brings us in touch with the transformative aspects of Integrated Movement. This is how magic works. One thing represents another, embodies it, becomes sacred by its use in ritual and healing. An object is sacred because of its usefulness and power. Without power, it had no value.

Participation is the key. You could even look at a blank canvas, and see the movies of your own mind. But this is not a passive activity, you must participate. You must bring yourself to the work physically. The body and mind must be willing to play the game, to enter, to feel, to relate.

In appreciating art, we need to access our physical feelings and reactions; the part of us that can scream, jump around, shake, throw a tantrum can also let us feel love, joy and be moved to tears. Our eyes are more than instruments of visual perception. They connect to our earliest bonding experience. Perhaps this visual bonding is the source of our feelings and responses to art.

Also at the turn of the century, as modern artists were exposed to tribal art and were presenting it to a new audience, Rudolf Laban, the creator of theories of movement and movement analysis, liberated movement from its stylized constraints. While Laban was an artist and performer, he also saw movement as a vital aspect of every part of life, dance, work, communication. He understood the value of movement in the community, for recuperation, for healing and for satisfaction in work. He defined effort dynamics, created scales of movement and acknowledged the therapeutic and spiritual nature of movement.

At the exhibit of primitive and modern work shown side by side at the Museum of Modern Art in New York City in 1984, I watched people involve their

Max Ernst, *The Interior of Sight: The Egg*

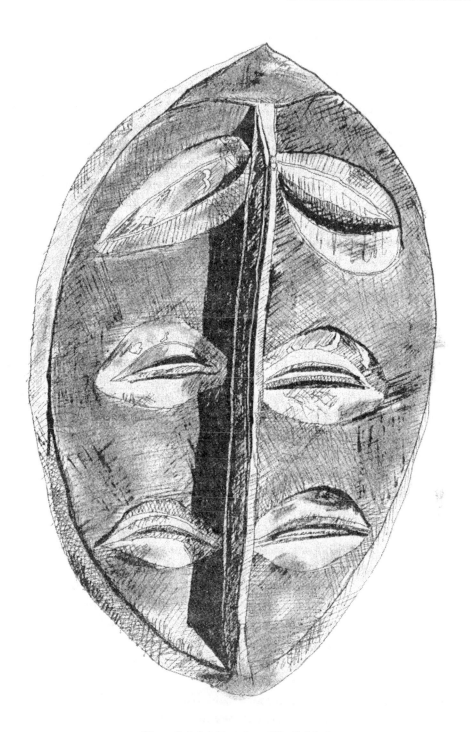

Steve Gabriel, Drawing of Kwele Mask

bodies in their communication while looking at the work. Just as a dialogue was established between each modern work and each tribal one, a dialogue was reflected in the discussion of the viewers. As people talked, they moved! They expressed feelings with their hands, voices and faces. One person followed the contours of a long smooth curve of a beautiful piece with her arm. Another made the movement of the dots of eyes, creating a dance step of the Easter Islands with the rhythm of her movement. People expressed their reactions to each other, relishing the meaning through their own movement.

There was quite a different mood in this exhibit from others. People seemed more aware of the physical space and shape of the room and of the presence of other people. We sensed each other differently. Strangers made connections to each other. We became a group having a similar experience. The power of the art was really working. The space became alive with a sense of communication.

THE SOUNDS OF CULTURE

We grow up hearing different sounds and rhythms and it affects our communication deeply. Rhythms of daily life tend to be repeated in music, dance and design. Just one example is the figure-eight carving movements of the rice cutters in Japanese fields reflected in the traditional Japanese fan dance movements.[1] Musicologist Alan Lomax, hypothesizes that child-rearing practices vary with rhythmic pattern, stricter practices having more regular beats.[8]

Voice overtones and vibrations, overlapping rhythms and harmonies can lead to unexpected integrations of sound. Bruce Gordon, guitarist and songwriter, explained to me how rhythm and melody can be integrated.

BG: *"Elvis Presley felt the rhythm in his voice, and showed it in his body. He sang the rhythm, which is a tradition in black music, but it was the first time white audiences heard the rhythm inside the melody. When Elvis sang, you could almost hear the drum in his voice and he couldn't sing without moving.*

"You can have a nice melody, and that's one thing. You can have a beat that makes you want to dance. You can put the nice melody over the beat and get away with it, but the ideal is to incorporate that nice melody into the beat, so that the words you sing will be the beat of the song. The Beatles were good at it. Crooners like Frank Sinatra and Bing Crosby were more concerned with melody than rhythm. Scat singers, tap dancers and rap artists accentuate rhythm. Gene Kelly and Fred Astaire mixed the two."

Musicians have a deep listening sense which engages the whole body. When they perform with conviction and skill, they move with Integrated Movement, communicating their understanding and expression of the music.

Denise Ayers is a violinist who has performed and toured with the New York Philharmonic Orchestra. The integrating concept of western music became very clear in a recent tour of the East. Since she was also trained in Laban Movement Analysis, she experienced everything about the culture through a sense of rhythm and sound.

DA: *"We played Mahler. You know, you need to do this big "swoosh" through your whole body to support the intensity you feel during his crescendo. It peaks with the force of the brass and strings behind the rest of the orchestra. Then, suddenly there's the let down to pianissimo. It's very Western, with its wave quality that pushes, then stops. Feeling the different rhythms and sounds around me, I experienced the differences in cultures."*

"In Japan, the focus is on the lower body. The feet move very fast; a quick, fast walk, low to the ground. The music has the same sinking under curve as the movement of the pelvis. There is a constant accommodation by weaving in and out, but there is never a sense of confrontation. No space is ignored. You simply have to anticipate what the other person is going to do.

"In Bangkok, the people live over and in the water. There are sudden showers. Rain sets up a rhythm. People stop and wait for the rain.

"In India the river flows like a central force through people's lives. The music organizes this way too and flows like a river. When you look around you see the juxtaposition between the lightness of the sky and the weight of the earth. You can see the rhythms and qualities of the sounds in everyday movements and in the movement of the environment. The clothing the women wore was draped and pleated around the body, enhancing fluidity of movement."

THE PERFORMER'S POINT OF VIEW

In order to recreate spontaneity despite memorized scripts, the actor studies movement carefully, then analyzes and draws on personal memories and images to allow a conscious shift into what appears to be an un-selfconscious moment.

A Dancer

Kathy, a professional folk dancer, described her movement as sometimes 'dry' and unengaging. She knew she had to change, but didn't know how. *"Hear your own breathing as you move,"* I counseled. *"First, move on the inhale, then on the exhale."* She used this breath technique not to control her movement, but to free her thought. By adding the lively dynamics and rhythms which were often a part of her movement, she became engrossed in the movement and so did the viewer. Yet, something was still missing.

I asked Kathy to describe her thought process as she moved. I suggested she concentrate on images, colors or landscapes. The change in her movement was dramatic. It had intent. It projected. I was suddenly spellbound. We did not have to work on Integrated Movement directly. For Kathy, it was a natural result of the depth of involvement she now experienced. She kept moving, saying; *"I've got it. I could keep moving forever!"*

A Storyteller

An experienced storyteller I know was very conscious of her own Integrated Movement. It was built into her style. The result was a sense that she was totally comfortable on stage and therefore made the audience comfortable. Her postures describing characters brought laughter. Her gestures amplified and punctuated her verbal statements. And, when it was appropriate, she responded to the images she created with Integrated Movements, as if she were the listener.

She connected stories of other cultures to her own. The words were extemporaneous and she would interrupt herself, then pick up the main thread. There was nothing artificial in her manner or in the content. As a result, the audience could get lost in the world of imagination she created.

An American Choreographer Of Balinese Dance

I.P.: *"When I rehearse, I never use a mirror, so there is no outside model. I do it very kinesthetically and try to sense a particular character.*

"I think the Balinese have an interesting way of integrating posture and gesture. I have noticed that taking their time and being approachable is part of the Balinese woman's nature. This calm quality towards the flow of time is inherent in the culture, intertwined in their myths, images and daily life."

Islene realized that the decelerating Integrated Movement she saw in the dance was the same graceful, steady movement Balinese women make when walking, even when balancing objects on their heads.

I.P.: *"When you are performing, the last thing you think about is how you are moving. Imagery takes over. That best describes my experience of Integrated Movement moments in rehearsal and in performance."*

ELEVEN

REFLECTIONS

Sensitivity to movement often leads us easily into a place of intuitive understanding which can at times seem psychic. Movement is a reflection of our inner selves. We become aware of the influence we have over our own thoughts and feelings, even over our lives. We begin to approach people differently, see ourselves differently, get different responses. We may even find ourselves listening to a 'voice' deep within, and able to make changes we didn't think possible.

Movement seems to me to be the fulcrum between visible and invisible experience, between form and idea, between body and mind. Movement is the visible part of thought. In studying movement, we invest in the descriptions and analysis of the ephemeral. Movement creates form.

As the balancing point between the body and the mind, movement can lead us into the tangible physical world of action and into the intangible spiritual world of metaphysics and healing. When we take an idea and make it happen, we have bridged the two worlds, spirit and form.

Every time someone discovers his own personal creativity, whether in healing the body, in communication, or artistically, a healing action has happened. Elements come together demonstrating wholeness.

Healing is the moment of renewal. A wound heals when the skin begins to regenerate, when the cells knit together. In a broken bone, the fibers grow, form new cells and create the lattice work which will again support weight and allow for full action. Energy flows through the broken parts. Great attention has been brought to bear in the process to allow healing to take place.

Why should it be any different from the process of healing emotions or psychological issues? We need active participation on both the body and mind level. To change, we have to separate ourselves from an idea we have always believed, a limitation, a dependence, a loss. These are painful separations. A new archetype, a new self-image has to emerge.

Yet, awareness alone will not change a pattern. An awareness that lets you change what you do, how you sit, how you speak, what you think, does. The body has to master the awareness in some way for the change to happen.

Movement encourages us to notice our environment, to become conscious of other people, other creatures. The Eastern concept of the Third Eye corresponds to the pituitary gland, the seat of self-perception. It perceives the self from within. It also perceives others. When we listen deeply to ourselves, we can hear others. These are adjacent skills we develop from the study of movement. We each have a little gem to which our consciousness is attached, our bodies. We sense what someone is thinking or feeling by his or her movement. Waves of energy accompany movement and sound. These waves are signals we learn to recognize.

The individual is a whole, but can't always see that whole. Just as we can't see the planet because we are on it, we can't see our whole experience, because we are in it. We are trying to understand ourselves from the inside. We break it all down to a vocabulary of gestures, of postures, of Integrated Movements, where we each try to tell each other who we are, what we think and what we feel.

As we listen to our inner selves in order to make our Integrated Movement conscious, we get in touch with goals and desires which are almost too big or cherished to admit. In our final exercise, listen deeply to your own dreams and wishes. Let the body lead you into a symbolic creation which allows you to integrate your unique dreams into your current changing reality.

MANIFEST YOUR GOAL

1. Imagine your ideal environment, in all aspects, physical conditions, work, people, everything.

2. Make the picture as glamorous as possible, as rich as possible, as nourishing as possible. Put in every detail you can imagine.

3. Create your reality purely for yourself. Others participate if they wish to. Have the feeling of the best of what you want with someone, but do not manipulate anyone in the process.

4. Draw, collage or build this dream. Create a picture until you find yourself entering a fantasy or remembering a place. Describe all that exists. Write key words. You may need a few minutes to quiet the thoughts going through your mind. Lie down. Breathe deeply, until an image comes to you. Use forms and color. You do not need to be realistic. Take time to study the picture. Be sure it has the essence of everything you can think of at the moment.

5. Notice the way you feel when you are describing your picture; the lovely meadow, the fruit trees, or the seashore with waves rolling in, the quaint farmhouse, or the New York penthouse where you are enjoying literary company as you work on your new play.

6. You may have many personal revelations as you do this work. Record these as they come. You may or may not want to share them, but they will be valuable for you. You are freeing yourself from attitudes /postures, and habits /gestures, which have limited you in the past, interfering with the creation of something which you want now and which you already have in essence.

7. When you are done, draw connections between what you now have and what you want. You will see how the seeds of what you want already exist in your present. You will now be allowing for solutions which previously might have seemed far off and impossible. Do not keep your dream outside yourself where it can continue to seem unattainable. See that it is already started in you, in your life.

EPILOGUE:
OUR QUANTUM LEAP

Having studied our communication from every angle, through emotional traumas, work problems, family frustrations, Pamela and I took a leap into the vast future. We tried to glimpse geological time to see how things would evolve:

Pamela: *"The universe is expanding. The sun is heating up on its way to becoming a red giant. That means everything in the universe is expanding."*

Ellen: *"Are we going to heat up and expand too?"*

Pamela: *"Why not? Do you remember how small the Egyptian statues we saw at the Metropolitan Museum were? Really tiny. Minute. About four feet six inches."*

Ellen: *"Are you saying we are bigger now because we are expanding?"*

Pamela: *"Yes, that's the theory."*

Ellen: *"Not vitamins? And you think we will keep expanding until we become less and less dense, which means we will be able to astral travel, move through space, find other planets with other suns which are not burning up? So we will evolve while our sun is evolving and it will all work out?*

"Is it the raisins in the pudding theory? As the universe expands, the planets and galaxies move apart. The gravitational pull between things decreases. As gravity reduces things get less and less dense."

We discussed this with a scientist who first made the distinction between density of structure and density of mind. We then went on to apples and grapes. Apples float and grapes sink. Strawberries float, tomatoes sink. Starch has a low density, a large volume for a given weight. Sugar has a higher density, (possibly explaining why grapes sink). To float, a molecule has to be larger than the water molecule. Then it displaces its own weight.

Ellen: *"In the planetarium you weigh yourself on different planets. If you weigh less on the moon, and stay there for a while, does your density decrease? (Hopefully, in both of your cases, says a 'friend.')"*

That's just what we thought could happen to us. Gradually, our bodies, mostly water, will weigh less as we heat up along with the sun, take up more space, again, like steam, and we will convert to another kind of cloud-like creature. We will be able to dematerialize and travel along. We will be as light as the insects. Maybe we will pass through a stage where we can fly and become isotopic, equally distributed throughout space. Interplanetary gravity keeps us all in orbit and that will decrease as the raisins move apart.

Pamela: *"What we really need to do is put ourselves into crystals and wait it out. Maybe getting more dense is the answer. Like the black holes. Well, we have some time to figure it out.*

"If we can't travel any other way, we can at least make space ships to float around the universe and find one of the hundred billion suns which is in its springtime. So our chance of being alive somewhere is pretty great."

Ellen: *"Maybe we will have learned to tesseract, and will be able to visit all but the two-dimensional planets. That would give us lots of options.*

"When we tesseract to travel in space, we will fold into ourselves structurally, we will shift between foreground and background, losing ourselves between the posture and gesture. This must be quite a shift in perception. Do you think this happens to the astronauts?"

Pamela: *"Yes. With no fixed point of reference they can change their perspective pretty well and get rid of lots of prejudice. Also, in the release from gravity, the cells expand, so they get that wonderful sense of confidence. (I know they grow about two inches.) Maybe their movement is global, like a child's, reacting with total involvement, but without the resistance of gravity."*

The most important aspect of the space program may be that it gave us a global world perspective, reminding us how much our senses tend to prescribe our world view. The global perspective is a kind of enlightenment to our role and purpose, an awareness of our importance and insignificance at once. Knowing both and living both fully is the enlightenment.

Ellen: *"The astronauts help us make the shift as we watch them on T.V. By identification, part of us goes with them. On the morning of a lift-off, I could feel that sunrise should be called 'sun-sighting' as Fuller recommends."*

Astro-physicists view remote galaxies as if it were many eons ago when they began making their long journey through space. They actually listen to the hum of the "big bang" and watch red and blue shifts of light to see how fast stars are moving. Our tools and instruments have taken us far into the macro and micro structures of the visible and invisible. Our humans skills do not yet equal our technological ones.

Pamela: *"Do you think we will be able to cope with planetary change? Will our evolution keep pace or will our chemistry be stuck in gravity, too solid, too thick and heavy? Will we be able to make ourselves comfortable in very hot temperatures, preparing for the cool down when we return to our dense selves?"*

Ellen: *"I can see us playing with matter, spinning it like spiders or knitting it like a sweater. Movement will then be irrelevant, used only when we dress up in "period costumes," our old bodies. We will instead communicate through ESP, using sound and light as the dance. We will dissolve and manifest as needed. Movement will be the dinosaur of expression. Maybe we will evolve slowly, becoming less dense, then liquify, then vaporize, while maintaining our uniqueness. Maybe we will learn to transform matter to antimatter and back, until we can become as dense as black holes and create new universes. Maybe we can crystallize back when we need a rest and become sparkling amethyst or quartz only to hop into action when needed or inspired, and space travel to our communities on other galaxies."*

Pamela: *"It's starting to sound like fun, although I might miss these familiar skeletons. I wonder how OTHERS WILL SEE US then?"*

Notes

Prologue

1. The Action Profiling® System was created by Warren Lamb from the teachings of Rudolf von Laban. To avoid cross-cultural influences, the movement which was observed was not a gesture or posture, but a blending of the two into a consistent quality or shape. At first, the movement was called a Posture/Gesture Merger. Later it was renamed Integrated Movement to reflect the moment of change. This aspect of movement is consistent over time and, when analyzed for its specific qualities and shapes, describes a pattern of thought and action called an Action Profile Assessment.

    Working closely with Warren Lamb, as his partner for many years in Warren Lamb Associates, Pamela Ramsden developed training methods for the system. I became her student, and later we explored new ways of using the Integrated Movement.

Chapter One

1. *Mind and Nature,* Gregory Bateson, (New York: Bantam Books, 1980), p. 34. See also Sections 4 and 5.
2. Museum of Modern Art, New York City, date unknown.
3. *Mind and Nature,* p. 38. Discussion of parallax.
4. R. Buckminster Fuller, *Critical Path*, (New York: St. Martin's Press, 1981) p. 55. "We do live on board an 8000 mile-in-diameter spherical spaceship speeding around the sun at 60,000 miles per hour, spinning axially as it orbits." p. 131, "Whether I am "in residence" or not, my land, my house, you too, and I whirl constantly around the earth's axis together (at about 800 miles per hour in the latitude of New York City), as all the while our little Spaceship Earth zooms around the Sun at 60,000 miles per hour, while at the same time our solar system rotates in its nebular merry-go-round at hundreds of thousands of miles per hour — none of which celestial-arena traveling did I include in my previously stated lifetime mileages or in those of other Earthians."
5. See non-verbal researchers, e.g., Scheflen, Condon, Kendon, Birdwhistell.

Chapter Two

1. Judith Kestenberg, M.D., *Children and Parents:Psychoanalytic Studies in Development* (New York: Jason Aronson, 1975).
2. Albert Scheflen, *How Behavior Means*, (New York: Jason Aronson, 1974), p. 142.
3. Susan Higgins, professor at Hunter College, presentation at Laban Institute: Tetanies.

Chapter Four

1. Locomotion, as defined by movement analysts, denotes movement which travels from one point to another.
2. Eye Workshop with Martha Eddy Spring, 1989

Chapter Five

1. Edward Hall, *Beyond Culture*. (New York: Anchor, 1977).
2. See Arnold Mindell, primary and secondary processes.
3. See "Unconscious Mental Functioning" by Joseph Weiss, *Scientific America*, March, 1990.
4. See *Wishcraft* by Barbara Sher (New York: Viking Press, 1979).

Chapter Six

1. Picture two snow fences which you can see overlapping. As you walk by them, a pattern of interference is created. The pattern is created by the spaces between them. A new pattern is created where they join. This is called a moiré pattern.
2. John Bradshaw, *Bradshaw On: The Family*. (Deerfield Beach, FL: Health Communications, 1988).
3. Of course you have to go beyond anger, blame and feelings of betrayal. One helpful resource is *Intimate Partners: Patterns in Love and Marriage* by Maggie Scarf.
4. Carl Jung, *Memories, Dreams and Reflections*. (New York: Random House, 1989).
5. We attribute the qualities we need to others in order to learn about them. We gradually incorporate our projections, strengthening ourselves as we go. When we cannot, we continue to project our needs and fail to see

how they relate to ourselves. Once we capture a projection and understand it, we do not need to project it. M. Esther Harding, *Way of All
Women* (New York: G. P. Putnam's Sons, 1970).

6.   Workshop guided by Aileen Crow, 1989.
7.   John Bradshaw, *Bradshaw On: The Family*.

Chapter Eight

1.   Although Integrated Movement is powerful and persuasive, it can not ensure the values or morals of an individual.

Chapter Nine

1.   See Kestenberg, Judith and Sossin, Mark, *Role of Movement Patterns in
Development,* (New York: Dance Notation Bureau Press, 1979), Volume
II.
2.   Excerpts from a movement workshop led by Bonnie Bainbridge Cohen,
New York City, December, 1984.
3.   There are many other associations to Chakras. Some authorities place
them in different relationship to the glands. Diane Stein's *The Women's
Book Of Healing* (St: Paul, MN: Llewellyn Publications, 1989) has a
good discussion of them; "The Rainbow Of The Chakras", p. 27.
      Information on the developmental patterns from Bonnie Bainbridge
Cohen's letter of March 10, 1993.

Chapter Ten

1.   Alan Lomax, *Dance and Human History*, Choreometrics Project (Berkeley:
University of California Media Center, c. 1974), (film and video).
2.   See "Maori Power" in *Natural History*, September 1984.
3.   See *Movement Patterns in Development II* by Dr. Judith Kestenberg.
4.   In the Metropolitan Museum of Art, New York, November 9, 1984.
5.   See Josef Albers, *Color Squares*.
6.   " *Primitivism" in 20th Century Art*, (New York: Museum of Modern Art,
1984), p.17. "That primitive art influenced Picasso and many of his colleagues in significant ways is beyond question. But that it caused no
fundamental change in the direction of modern art is equally true."
7.   From exhibit, Museum of Modern Art, Primitive Exhibit, 1984.
8.   See Alan Lomax article in *Interaction Rhythms* by Martha Davis (New
York: Human Sciences Press, 1982).

PHOTO CREDITS

Cover: Live-size bronze sculpture titled, *Sharing the Headlines*, by J. Seward Johnson, Jr.

Photo courtesy of Sculpture Placement, Ltd. Washington, DC

Life-size bronze sculptures by J. Seward Johnson, Jr.
Photos courtesy of Sculpture Placement, Ltd. Washington, DC

P. 8 *No Hands*
P. 13 *Sidewalk Judge*
P. 21 *Crack The Whip*
P. 61 *Chance Meeting*
P. 62 *News*
P. 80 *Big Sister*
P. 92 *Hell, Time to go Fishing*
P. 146 *The Right Light*
P. 148 *Taxi*

P. 122 Condyles of the Knee, Artists Drawing
P. 149 Claes Oldenburg, Installation at the Green Gallery, New York, September 24-October 20, 1962, including pieces from *The Store* and the first large-scale "soft" sculptures. Photograph by Rudolph Burckhardt.
P. 156 Erich Lessing/Art Resource, NY Vincent van Gogh, *Wheat and Cypress Trees*, 1889. National Gallery, London.
P. 158 Foto Marburg/Art Resource, NY Vincent van Gogh, *Les Alicamps*. Rijksmuseum Kroeller-Mueller, Otterlo, The Netherlands.
P. 160 Bridgeman/Art Resource, NY Vincent van Gogh, *Pollard Willows with Setting Sun*. Rijksmuseum Kroeller-Mueller, Otterlo, The Netherlands.
P. 161 Giraudon/Art Resource, NY Vincent van Gogh, *Self Portrait*, 1889. Musée d'Orsay, Paris.
P. 162 Art Resource, NY Paul Gauguin, *Arcarea, or les Joyeusettes*. Musée d'Orsay, Paris.

P. 164   The Menil Collection, Houston. Max Ernst, *A l'Intérieur de la vue : l'œuf*,
         © 1994 Artists Rights Society (ARS), New York/SPADEM, Paris. Photo-
         graph by Allen Mewbourn.

P. 165   Steve Gabriel, artist rendering of Kwele Mask, People's Republic of the
         Congo.

BIOGRAPHICAL SKETCHES OF LEADING MOVEMENT THEORISTS WHOSE INNOVATIVE WORK FORMS THE BASIS OF THIS BOOK:

RUDOLF VON LABAN

Rudolf von Laban's contribution to the understanding of movement is unparalleled. His extensive work reached beyond the traditional boundaries of dance and theater to industry. Laban's background included staging events for craft guilds, directing the Berlin opera, and designing theaters. He established numerous schools of movement throughout Germany before World War II, and with the help of his student Mary Wigman, shaped German Modern Dance.

Using his training in architecture, Laban conceptualized a way to represent human movement in three-dimensional space. The scales of movement he created became a new way to train the body for range of motion for sports and dance. Labanotation, a script for reading movement which he developed, elevated movement to the status of the written word.

Laban used the physical principles of weight, space, time and flow to analyze the dynamic range of the body's movement. He represented the qualities of human expression in an ingenious way, allowing for a deeper understanding of movement and a form of 'movement thinking.'

Later his ideas of movement education became established in the entire British school system.

WARREN LAMB

After Warren Lamb left the British Navy, he met Rudolf Laban, studied with him for three years at the Art Of Movement Studio, then assisted him in his work in industry.

Lamb's work was nearly as diversified as Laban's. He became involved in theater, dance, and management consulting. He pioneered the development of the Action Profile® Assessment, also known as Movement Pattern Analysis. Using an understanding of people's everyday movement, and relating it to decision-making, he found a way to enhance job performance and job satisfaction.

Mr. Lamb now councils senior business executives, and supports the development of effective management teams. He is in demand world-wide as a consultant, lecturer, teacher.

IRMGARD BARTENIEFF

As a dancer, Irmgard Bartenieff began studying with Laban in Germany in 1925. She came to New York in 1936 and was one of the people who introduced Labanotation to this country. A physical therapist and one of the first dance therapists, she applied Laban's principles to her work, making a unique contribution to both fields.

Irmgard became known to anthropologists and non-verbal researchers for her understanding of movement. Margaret Mead sent people interested in dance ethnology to her. Ray Birdwhistell also referred people to her for a wider scope of interpretation. She collaborated with Alan Lomax on the film, *DANCE AND HUMAN HISTORY*. She worked at Bronx State Hospital in New York, where she influenced many psychiatrists and psychologists.

In 1965, she founded the Laban Movement Analysis department of the Dance Notation Bureau. In 1978 it became the Laban/Bartenieff Institute of Movement Studies, now on 11 East 4th street in Manhattan. Here she continued to teach Laban's concepts and her synthesis of these ideas in cross-cultural studies, education, dance, art therapies, martial arts, and the healing of injuries and chronic physical problems.

DR. JUDITH KESTENBERG

Dr. Judith Kestenberg was referred to Irmgard Bartenieff when she was looking for a way to analyze and understand the movement of babies. They became close friends and colleagues. Irmgard taught Dr. Kestenberg Laban's theories of movement, and Dr. Kestenberg applied them to her work in child psychoanalysis.

In 1955 they traveled to England for additional Laban movement training. There they studied with Warren Lamb whose movement profile Dr. Kestenberg adopted and developed into the Kestenberg Movement Profile. Her system has a movement parallel for every stage of child development. It allows the study of children and interaction patterns with parents.

Dr. Kestenberg is a former clinical professor of psychiatry and a training analyst at New York University. She was a founding member of The Child Development Research Center in Sands Point Long Island, where she developed and used the Kestenberg Movement Profile to assist the psychological development of children. Many art and dance therapists have interned at the Center. Today, her work is considered crucial to many dance therapy programs.

In addition, Dr. Kestenberg is the project director for the International Study of Organized Persecution of Children.

PAMELA RAMSDEN

After completing the course of study in Laban's work at the Art Of Movement Studio in England, Pamela Ramsden joined Warren Lamb, as a psychologist, with the goal of validating his Action Profile Assessment. She later apprenticed to him, became a business partner, and developed a training program for professionals working with the Action Profile System. Over the years, Pamela has influenced the development of new aspects of the System. She is a founding member and Vice President of Action Profilers International.

For the last thirteen years, she has been a partner in Decision Development, a consulting practice based in London, which specializes in developing executive potential, team-building and organizational skills.

BONNIE BAINBRIDGE COHEN

Bonnie Bainbridge Cohen began her career as an Occupational Therapist, trained at Ohio State University. She was certified as a Neurodevelopment Therapist by English specialists Dr. and Mrs. Bobath. Her interests reached to the practice of Zen, marital arts, Ideokinesis, voice study, dance therapy, and other relevant systems. In each, she worked with leaders in the field. Bonnie brought this varied background to her movement teaching in which the life of the body, its function, cells, organs, became the fabric of experience and expression.

The Laban approach has considerable impact in her work. Bonnie worked closely with Irmgard Bartenieff at the Laban Institute. She was certified in Laban Movement Analysis, the Kestenberg Movement Profile and completed the Introduction to the Action Profiling System.

Bonnie brings a world of understanding to even the simplest movement and experiences it on the deepest level, making connections to mind, thought and spirit. She works with the form and function of the body, and its application to human development, personal experience, and the life of the community.

Along with a private practice, she and her husband founded the School for Body/Mind Centering, in 1973, in Amherst Massachusetts, where she has been able to further develop her own unique synthesis of movement training and to certify others as practitioners of Body/Mind Centering.

ELLEN GOLDMAN'S CONNECTION TO THESE LEADING THEORISTS:

Beatrice Stronstorff Lees introduced Ellen to the art of improvisation and to the work of Rudolf Laban. In 1974, Ellen became a Certified Movement Analyst, having studied Laban Movement Analysis with Irmgard Bartenieff. Laban's spatial scales inspired her professional choreography and performances.

At the Laban Institute, she became aware of the work of Warren Lamb and Dr. Judith Kestenberg. Ellen met Bonnie Bainbridge Cohen in the Certification Program and began studying with her shortly thereafter.

In 1978 she studied the Action Profiling® System and applied it in recruiting, career development and management consulting. Working closely with Pamela Ramsden, Ellen became an Advanced Trainer and Standard Observer in the Action Profiling System.

In order to complete her background in the Laban Assessment techniques, she studied and qualified in the Kestenberg Movement Profile. She collaborated with Dr. Kestenberg in further research into the Laban scales of movement and how they describe communication, now available in The Geometry of Movement, Part 1 and 2.

Ellen's association with Pamela Ramsden in designing training programs, developed into a collaboration on a new application for the Integrated Movement feature of the Action Profile System.

For many years, Ellen Goldman has been teaching in the Year-Long Certification Program at the Laban Institute. She blends the work of the Kestenberg Movement Profile, the Action Profile and Laban Movement Analysis as an independent consultant in New York City.

Bibliography

Argyle, Michael. *Bodily Communication*. 2nd ed. London and New York: Methuen & Co., Ltd., 1988.

Arnheim, Rudolph. *Art and Visual Perception*. Berkeley: University of California Press, 1954.

——————.*Visual Thinking*. Berkeley: University of California Press, 1969.

Bardi, Patricia and Gail Turner, eds. Research by Bonnie Bainbridge Cohen, Amherst: School for Body/Mind Centering, 1977.

Bartenieff, Irmgard. *Body Movement / Coping with the Environment*. New York and London: Gordon and Breach, 1980.

Basmajian. *Grant's Method of Anatomy*. 9th ed. Baltimore: Williams & Wilkins Co., 1975.

Bateson, Gregory. *Mind and Nature*. New York: Bantam Books, 1979.

Bateson, Mary Catherine, *With a Daughter's Eye*. New York: William Morrow & Co., 1984.

Birdwhistell, Ray L. *Kinesics and Context*. Philadelphia: University of Pennsylvania Press, 1970.

"Body Language for Business Success," New York: National Institute of Business Management Inc., 1988.

Bradshaw, John E. *Bradshaw On: The Family: A Revolutionary Way of Self Discovery*. Deerfield Beach, FL: Health Communications, 1988.

Csikszentmihalyi, Mihaly. *Flow: The Psychology of Optimal Experience*. New York: Harper & Row, 1990.

Darwin, Charles. *The Express of Emotions in Man and Animals*. Chicago: University of Chicago Press, 1965.

Davis, Martha, ed. *Interaction Rhythms*. New York: Human Sciences Press, 1982.

Fast, Julius. *The Body Language of Sex, Power and Aggression*. New York: Jove, 1978.

——————.*Body Language*, New York: Pocket Book, 1970.

Ferber, Jane, Beels, Chris and Schoonbeck, John. "Construct Analysis of a Family Interview," unpublished monograph and video, Philadelphia: University of Pennsylvania Film Library.

Freedman, Norbert, Van Meel, J. M., Barroso, F., and Bucci, W. "On the Development of Communicative Competence," *Semiotica* 62 (1986): pp. 77-105.

Freedman, Norbert and Steingart, I. "Kinesic Internalization and Language Construction," *Semiotica*.

Fuller, Buckminster. *Ideas and Integrities*. New York: Collier Books, 1963.

——————. *Critical Path*, New York: St. Martin's Press, 1981.

——————. *Modeling the Universe*,(Film), Pyramid Film.

Gavin, James. *Body Moves*. Harrisburg, PA: Stackpole Books, 1988

Goldberg, Herb. *The New Male-Female Relationship*. New York: Morrow, 1983.

Goldman, Ellen. "The KMP Contribution to the Defense Scale and Communication," *The Kestenberg Movement Profile: Its Past, Present Applications and Future Directions*. Keene, ME: Antioch New England Graduate School, 1990.

Goldman, Ellen; Kestenberg, J.; Maloney, J.; Sherman, D.; and Walker, P. *The Defense Scale in Communication*. New York: Laban/Bartenieff Institute for Movement Studies, 1988.

Goleman, Daniel. "Non-Verbal Cues are Easy to Misinterpret." *New York Times*, September 17, 1991.

Goleman, Daniel. "Black Scientist Study the 'Pose' of the Inner City." *New York Times*, April 21, 1992.

Hall, Edward T. *The Dance of Life*. New York: Anchor, .

——————. *Beyond Culture*, New York: Anchor, 1977.

——————. *The Silent Language*. New York: Anchor, 1973.

——————. *The Hidden Dimension*. New York: Anchor, 1969.

Hanna, Judith Lynne. *To Dance is Human: A Theory of Nonverbal Communication*. Austin and London: University of Texas Press, 1987.

Harding, M. Esther. *The Way of All Women*.

Harms, William. "McNeill: Gestures reveal 'a new dimension of mind'." *The University of Chicago Chronicle*, April 16, 1992.

Henley, Nancy. *Body Politics: Power, Sex and Nonverbal Communication*. Englewood Cliffs, NJ: Prentice-Hall, 1977.

Jung, Carl G. *Memories, Dreams and Reflections*. New York: Random House, 1989.

Kestenberg, Judith. *Children and Parents: Psychoanalytic Studies in Development*. New York: Jason Aronson, 1975.

Kestenberg, Judith. *The Role of Movement Patterns in Development*. vol. I. New York: The Dance Notation Bureau Press, 1977.

Kestenberg, Judith and Sossin, Mark. *The Role of Movement Patterns in Development II*. New York: The Dance Notation Bureau Press, 1979.

Laban, Rudolf. *The Mastery of Movement*. Plymouth: McDonald & Evans, 1950.

—————. *The Language of Movement: A Guidebook to Choreutics*. Massachusetts: Plays, Inc., 1974.

Laing, R.D. *The Voice of Experience*. New York: Pantheon Books, 1982.

Lamb, Warren. *Posture and Gesture*. London: Duckworth & Co., 1965.

Lamb, Warren and Watson, Elizabeth. *Body Code: The Meaning in Movement*. London: Routledge & Kegan Paul, 1979.

Lewis, Penny and Loman, Susan. *The Kestenberg Movement Profile: Its Past, Present Applications and Future Directions*. Keene, ME: Antioch New England Graduate School, 1990.

Loman, Susan, ed. *The Body-Mind Connection in Human Movement Analysis*. Keene, ME: Antioch New England Graduate School, 1992.

Lomax, Alan. *Folk Song, Style and Culture*. Washington, D.C.: American Association for the Advancement of Science, 1968.

Lomax, Alan; Bartenieff, Irmgard; Paulay, Forrestine; and Arensberg, Conrad. *Dance and Human History* (Film), Choreometrics Project, 1974

Lomax, Alan and Paulay, Forrestine. *Rhythms of Dances: Step Styles* (Film), Choreometrics Project, 1987.

"Maori Power." *Natural History*, 9/84.

McMinn, R.M.H. and Hutchings, R.T. *Color Atlas of Human Anatomy*. Chicago: Medical Publishers Inc., 1977.

McNeill, David. "So You Think Gestures Are Nonverbal?," *Psychological Review* no. 3 (1985), pp. 350-371.

Mills, Margaret and Cohen, Bonnie Bainbridge. *Manual. Amherst: School for Body/Mind Centering.* 1979.

Mindell, Arnold. *The River's Way.* New York and London: Routledge & Kegan Paul, 1985.

Moore, Carol-Lynne and Yamamoto, Kaoru. *Beyond Words.* New York and London: Gordon & Breach, 1988.

Morris, Desmond. *The Naked Ape.* New York: Dell, 1984.

Nierenberg, Gerald and Calero, Henry. *How to Read a Person Like a Book.* New York: Pocket Book, 1971.

Pease Allan, *Signals.* New York: Bantam Books, 1984.

Rico, Gabriele Lusser. *Writing the Natural Way.* Los Angeles: J.P. Tarcher Press, 1983.

Rudolph, Ellen. "Women's Talk," *New York Times Magazine*, September 1, 1991.

Saner-Yiu, Raymond. "Psychological Movement Patterns in Psychotherapy," *Human Movement Science* 4 (1985): 67-86.

Scarf, Maggie. *Intimate Partners: Patterns in Love and Marriage.* New York: Ballantine, 1987.

Scheflen, Albert E. *How Behavior Means.* New York: Jason Aronson, 1974.

————. *Body Language and the Social Order.* Englewood Cliffs, NJ: Prentice-Hall, 1972.

Shawn, Ted. *Every Little Movement—A book About Francois Delsarte.* New York: Dance Horizons, 1968.

Sher, Barbara. *Wishcraft.* New York: Viking Press, 1979.

Stein, Diane. *The Woman's Book of Healing.* St. Paul, MN: Llewellyn Publications, 1989.

Todd, Mabel Elsworth. *The Thinking Body.* New York: Dance Horizons, 1937.

Winter, Deborah D.; Widell, C.; Truitt, G.; Shields, T.; and George-Falvey, J. "Empirical Studies of Posture-Gesture Mergers." *Journal of Nonverbal Behavior*, 1989, pp. 207-223.

Ueland, Brenda. *If You Want to Write.* St. Paul: Graywolf Press, 1987.

Weinstein, Marion. *Positive Magic: Occult Self-Help*. Custer: Phoenix Publishing, 1981.

Weiss, Joseph. "Unconscious Mental Functioning," *Scientific American*, March 1990, pp. 103-109.

Weitz, Shirley, ed. *Nonverbal Communication*. New York: Oxford University Press, 1979.

Younger, Eric. "Hopi Photographers/Hopi Images." *Natural History*, May 1984.

Zukov, Gary. *The Dancing Wuli Masters*. New York: Morrow Quill, 1979.

Further Readings in Non-Verbal Communication

Bauml, Betty J. and Baumi, Franz H. *A Dictionary of Gesture*. Metuchen, NJ: Scarecrow Press, 1975.

Beattie, Geoffry. *Talk: An Analysis of Speech and Non-Verbal Behavior in Conversation*. Bristol, PA: Open University Press, 1983.

Blanck, Peter D. *Nonverbal Communication in the Clinical Context*. State College, PA: Pennsylvania State University Press, 1986.

Breasure, Joyce M. C. *Nonverbal Communication in Skills Handbook*. Tampa: Advanced Development Systems, Inc., 1982.

Brodey, Warren. *Earthchild: Glories of the Asphyxiated Spectrum*, New York: Gordon & Breach, 1974.

Brown, Charles T. and Keller, Paul T. *Monologue to Dialogue: An Exploration of Inter-Personal Communication*. Englewood Cliffs, NJ: Prentice Hall, 1979.

Bull, Paul. *Posture and Gesture*. New York: Pergamon Press, 1987.

————. *Body Movement and Inter-Personal Communication*. 1983.

Bullowa, Margaret. *Before Speech*. Cambridge: Cambridge University Press, 1979.

Burgoon, Judee K. and Saine, Thomas. *The Unspoken Dialogue: An Introduction to Nonverbal Communication*. New York: Harper College, 1978.

Caro, Mike. *Mike Caro's Book of Tell's: Poles Body Language*. New York: Gambling Times, Distributed by the Carol Publishing Group, 1984.

Cooper, Ken. *Body Business: The Sender's and Receiver's Guide to Nonverbal Communication*. Total Communication Publishing, 1981.

Davis, Martha. *Understanding Body Movement: An Annotated Bibliography*. Manchester, NH: Ayer Press, 1971.

Davis, Martha and Skupier, Janet. *Body Movement and Nonverbal Communication: An Annotated Bibliography*. Manchester, NH: Ayer Press, 1975.

Delmar, Ken. *Winning Moves: The Body Language of Selling*. New York: Warner Books, 1985.

Donaghy, William C. *Our Silent Language: An Introduction to Nonverbal Communication.* 1980.

Ellgring, Heiner. *Non-Verbal Communication in Depression.* Cambridge: Cambridge University Press, 1989.

Emmert, Philip and Donaghy, William C. *Human Communication: Elements and Contexts.* New York: McGraw-Hill Book Co., 1981.

Fast, Julius and Fast, Barbara. *Talking Between Lines.* New York: Viking Press, 1979

Frandsen and Benson. *Nonverbal Communication.* 1984.

Frey, D. *Analyzing Patterns of Behavior in Dyadic Interaction.* Kirkland, WA: Hogrefe and Huber Publishers, .

Hall, Judith A. *Nonverbal Sex Differences: Communicating Accuracy and Expressive Style.* Baltimore: Johns Hopkins University Press, 1984.

Haper, Robert G. *Nonverbal Communication: The State of the Art.* 1978.

Heisel, D. *The Kairos Dimension.* New York: Gordon & Breach, 1974.

Hickson, III., Mark L. *Nonverbal Communication Studies and Applications.* Madison, WI: Brown & Benchmark, 1989.

Hinde, R. A., ed. *Nonverbal Communication.* Cambridge: Cambridge University Press, 1972.

Katz, Albert M. and Katz, Virginia T. *Foundations of Nonverbal Communication: Readings, Examples, and Commentary.* Carbondale: Southern Illinois University Press, 1983.

Kendon, Adam. *Nonverbal Communication, Interaction and Gesture.* Hawthorne, NY: Mouton Publisher, 1981.

Key, Mary R. *Paralanguage and Kinesics: Nonverbal Communication with Annotated Bibliography. Metuchen, NJ:* Scarecrow Press, 1975.

——————. *Nonverbal Communication Today.* Hawthorn, NY: Mouton Publisher, 1982.

——————. *The Relation of Verbal and Nonverbal Communication.* 1982.

Kleinke, Chris. *Meeting and Understanding People,* First Impressions. Englewood Cliffs, NJ: Prentice Hall, 1986.

Knapp, Mark L. *Essentials of Nonverbal Communication.* New York: Holt Rinehart & Winston, 1980.

Leathers, Dale A. *Successful Nonverbal Communication: Principles and Applications*. New York: Macmillan, 1986.

Machotka, Parel and Spiegel, John P. *Articulate Body*. New York: Irvington Publishers, 1982.

Malandro, Loretta A. and Barker, Larry L. *Introduction to Nonverbal Communication*. New York: McGraw-Hill Book Co., 1982.

Malandro, Loretta A. *Nonverbal Communication*, New York: McGraw-Hill Book Co., 1988.

Mayo, C. and Henley, N. H. *Gender and Nonverbal Communication* (Behavior). New York: Springer Verlag Publishers, 1981.

Mehrabian, Albert. *Nonverbal Communication*. Chicago: Aldine-Atherton, 1972.

Merdel, D. *Proper Doctoring*. New York: Springer Verlag Publishers, 1982.

Molcho, Sumy. *Body Speech*. New York: St. Martins Press, 1985.

Noller, P. *Nonverbal Communication and Marital Interaction*. New York: Pergamon Press, 1984.

Obudho, Constance E. *Human Nonverbal Communication: An Annotated Bibliography*. Westport, CT: Greenwood Press, 1979.

Pairio, Allan. *Mental Representations: A Dual Coding Approach*. New York: Oxford University Press, 1990.

Patterson, M. L. *Nonverbal Behavior*. New York: Springer Verlag, 1983.

Reilly, Abigail. *The Communication Game: Perspectives on the Development of Speech, Language and Nonverbal Communication Skills*. Skillman, NJ: J&J Consumer Products, 1980.

Rosenthal, Robert. *Sensitivity to Nonverbal Communication: The Pons Test*. Baltimore: Johns Hopkins University Press, 1979.

————. *Skill in Nonverbal Communication: Individual Differences*. Baltimore: Johns Hopkins University Press, 1979.

Ruesch, Jurgen and Kees, Weldon. *Nonverbal Communication: Notes on the Visual Perception of Human Relations*. Berkeley: University of California Press, 1956.

Rutter, Derek. *Looking and Seeing: The Role of Visual Communication in Social Interaction*. New York: John Wiley, 1984.

Scherer, Klaus R. and Ekman, Paul, eds. *Handbook of Methods in Nonverbal Behavior Research*. Cambridge: Cambridge University Press,

Schiefelbusch, R. *Nonspeech Language and Communication*. Baltimore: University Park Press, 1982.

Siegman, Aron W. and Feldstein, Stanley, eds. *Nonverbal Behavior and Communication*, Hillsdale, NJ: L. Eribaum Assoc. distributed by Halsted Press, 1987.

Stacks, Donald. *Exploring Nonverbal Communication*. 1985.

Subach, Marilyn B. *The 60 Second Impression: What You Have Said Before You Say "Hello,"* Phoenix: Classic Consultants, 1985.

Trombetta, John J. *Workbook for Nonverbal Communication*. Dybbuk, IA: Kendall Hunt, 1985.

Van Schaak, M. *Without Words: An Introduction to Nonverbal Communication*, Cambridge, MA: P.H. Press, 1977.

Vargas, Marjorie F. *Louder Than Words: An Introduction to Nonverbal Communication*. Ames: Iowa State University Press, 1986.

Von Ruffler-Engel, Waburga, ed. *Aspects of Nonverbal Communication*. Bristol, PA: Swets Publishers, Service, Taylor and Francis, 1980.

Walmsley, Gordon. *Kinesis*. New York: Bridgehead Press, 1983.

Webbink, Patricia. *The Power of the Eyes*. New York: Springer Verlag, 1986.

Weimann, John M. and Harrison, Randall P. *Nonverbal Interaction*. 1983.

Wolfgang, Aaron. *Nonverbal Behavior: Perspectives, Applications and Intercultural Insights*. Kirkland, WA: Hogrefe & Huber Publishing, 1984.

(Compiled by Jill David and Linda Jantz)

Index

Lightning Source UK Ltd.
Milton Keynes UK
UKOW05f1853280514

232473UK00007B/187/P